RACHEL JO

TIME TO Think²

THE THINGS THAT STOP OUR TEAMS AND WHAT TO DO ABOUT THEM

JOHN CATT
FROM HODDER EDUCATION

Every effort has been made to trace all copyright holders, but if any have been inadvertently overlooked, the Publishers will be pleased to make the necessary arrangements at the first opportunity.

Although every effort has been made to ensure that website addresses are correct at time of going to press, Hodder Education cannot be held responsible for the content of any website mentioned in this book. It is sometimes possible to find a relocated web page by typing in the address of the home page for a website in the URL window of your browser.

Hachette UK's policy is to use papers that are natural, renewable and recyclable products and made from wood grown in well-managed forests and other controlled sources. The logging and manufacturing processes are expected to conform to the environmental regulations of the country of origin.

Orders: please contact Hachette UK Distribution, Hely Hutchinson Centre, Milton Road, Didcot, Oxfordshire, OX11 7HH. Telephone: +44 (0)1235 827827. Email education@hachette.co.uk. Lines are open from 9 a.m. to 5 p.m., Monday to Friday.

ISBN: 9781036004811

© Rachel Johnson 2024

First published in 2024 by
John Catt from Hodder Education,
An Hachette UK Company
15 Riduna Park, Station Road,
Melton, Woodbridge IP12 1QT

www.johncatt.com

All rights reserved. Apart from any use permitted under UK copyright law, no part of this publication may be reproduced or transmitted in any form or by any means, electronic or mechanical, including photocopying and recording, or held within any information storage and retrieval system, without permission in writing from the publisher or under licence from the Copyright Licensing Agency Limited. Further details of such licences (for reprographic reproduction) may be obtained from the Copyright Licensing Agency Limited, www.cla.co.uk

A catalogue record for this title is available from the British Library

Time to Think 2 is the perfect follow on to the first book, exploring many of the issues that crop up in leadership and can stop our teams from functioning. Each aspect is unpicked and explored from different angles, providing a variety of practical solutions that can easily be adapted and trialled. *Time to Think 2* really encourages you to look at yourself as a leader and consider the kind of team that you want to lead. Like the first book, it is broken down into manageable bitesize chunks that are easy to dip in and out of, providing plenty of opportunities for reflection along the way. It promotes being both responsible and daring, outlines strategies to achieve this, and explores how to strike the right balance. There is something for everyone in this book.

Hannah Lee, Teacher and Raising Standards Leader

Leaders often describe themselves as time-poor; the *Time to Think* books help to solve this problem! Rachel has done the reading for you. She has taken the best leadership books, made the content relevant for school leaders and left you with the task of identifying what you and your team need and selecting the right tools to address that. Thank you, Rachel!

Laura Thompson, Assistant Headteacher

An absolute toolkit for leaders at all levels of schools and multi academy trusts. Beautifully researched, thoughtfully written and eminently practical to ensure the most impactful school cultures for our students.

Ben Wilcox, Assistant Headteacher and DSL

Thank you, Rachel, for making the time to write a second *Time to Think* book! It is packed full of leadership guidance from a variety of different sources to give the busy school leader the opportunity to reflect on their leadership. The part that really resonated with me was 'How to get into deep work'; Rachel says herself that this book only came into being due to 'Monk Mode Mondays' and it's definitely an approach that will form part of my working week in the future. It was also a pleasure to be part of Rachel's 'Big Think' online, which enabled a group of school leaders to see how powerful 'Group Brainstorming Online' really is for generating ideas in response to some thought-provoking questions.

Chris Stephens, Deputy Headteacher

An enjoyable, interesting read. If you are looking for one place to find a plethora of accessible research about leadership then this is a great starting point. I particularly liked Rachel's use of 'and' from the Lego paradoxes to reflect on leadership principles – it really shows the impact of such a small word – a definite 'time to think' moment. The 'head space' section at the end of each chapter is a wonderful opportunity to pause and reflect; to remind ourselves that we need head space as leaders to make informed decisions.

Joanne Stuart, Trust Development Lead, DHT

As with the first instalment, *Time to Think 2* balances relevant leadership theory with realistic, practical strategies that can be implemented by school leaders. I really value books that give you 'lightbulb moments' where you can suddenly see the how/why behind scenarios; this book has them in abundance.

Anna Heaven, Assistant Headteacher and RSL

Whether you're a seasoned leader or aspiring to take on a leadership role, *Time to Think 2* offers a practical guide filled with actionable strategies to help you navigate the complexities of team dynamics and lead with confidence. It's a must-read for anyone committed to unlocking the full potential of their team.

Sarah Judge, Vice Principal

To Charlotte, Daniel and Matthew,
I hope you experience the joy of being part of brilliant teams,
at school, at home and at work.

CONTENTS

INTRODUCTION

Leading ourselves is hard: being in control of ourselves, having boundaries, saying no, facing the brutal facts (while still having hope) and mastering crucial conversations are some of the biggest issues many of us struggle with. In the first *Time to Think*, I addressed all of these issues and more. Mastering those issues is the key to becoming the leader you want to be and there is no short cut; you have to do that work on yourself. Many of you are doing just that.

This book is about your *leadership* but also about your *followership*. We have to be the kind of leaders that people want to follow. The obstacles that stop people wanting to follow us can be wide and complex and although we all try to navigate our way through them successfully it is helpful to explore some of the common issues that come up in school leadership.

In this book, we are going to deal with some of the trickiest issues in leading a team. These issues are often not talked about although they are in plain sight. Even with issues we *do* know about, we might not know *what* to do, *why* we have to do it, or what the evidence says about *how* to do it best. This book aims to cut through the noise and bring you practical solutions and ideas that you can think about, adapt, and try.

Before we dive in though, first we need to reflect on the kind of team we want to lead. The leadership of teams will involve living in the heart of a range of paradoxes as we try to balance the people, the plans, and the approach. These paradoxes are not always comfortable, but we need to be leaders who say 'both/and' and not 'either/or'. This takes some practice especially in a world which can be so polarized at times.

On the wall of the Lego Museum are the paradoxes that Lego live by. It is a great list that reflects the nuanced nature of building and leading a team. The word 'and' does a lot of heavy lifting in all of these statements.

The 11 Lego Paradoxes:

1. To be able to establish close relationship with your employees and to keep proper distance.
2. To be able to take the lead, and to hold oneself in the background.
3. To trust one's staff, and to keep an eye on what is happening.
4. To be tolerant, and to know how you want things to function.
5. To keep the goals of one's department in mind, and at the same time be loyal to the whole firm.
6. To do a good job of planning your own time, and to be flexible with your schedule.
7. To freely express your view, and to be diplomatic.
8. To be a visionary, and to keep one's feet on the ground.
9. To try to win consensus, and to be able to cut through.
10. To be dynamic, and to be reflective.
11. To be sure of yourself, and to be humble.

It is helpful to come up with something similar regarding our own teams in schools. What is it we are trying to do and what are the paradoxes at play for us? You may find it isn't this *or* that, it is *both* this *and* that.

In her brilliant book *Ruthlessly Caring*, Amy Walters Cohen writes about embracing paradoxes and being 'future fit leaders'. She defines this as follows: 'Future-fit leaders are not perfect, nor are they completely "integrated" in every way (as integration is a process that never ends) – but they are comfortable operating with beliefs, attitudes, and values that *seem* contradictory'. We have to navigate seemingly contradictory things on a regular basis – like warm and strict, care and challenge, being tough on standards but kind on people.

Cohen suggests a number of leadership paradoxes in her work, but my favourite is 'responsibly daring'. Responsible leaders hold themselves accountable for making a difference to their workplace and its health, both in the present and in the future. They focus on the art of the possible and seek to find solutions to problems. They aim to serve their stakeholders. Daring leaders are optimistic about the future; they think creatively and innovatively, they take risks, experiment, and are brave in doing so.

We need to be both responsible *and* daring. If we are too responsible, we may become paralysed and avoid making changes that we know we need to make but don't feel brave enough to embrace. If we are too daring, we may become reckless in our pursuit of a goal and run into trouble, enjoying the excitement ourselves but striking fear into others! To be both responsible and daring means that we are open to other ideas, as well as being brave and innovative, while at the same time making a difference, taking the job seriously, and wanting to ensure that the organisation is healthy now and in the future. We take calculated risks. We listen to others. We don't get carried away with our own ideas without checking them out with others. We are brave. We feel safe enough to try. We stretch for things just outside of our reach. We are comfortable with being a little uncomfortable sometimes!

I hope this book helps you become both more responsible and more daring in your leadership of your teams. It will not be simple – leading people rarely is – but it will be worth it.

CHAPTER 1:
HOW TO GET 'BUY IN'

WHY DOES THIS MATTER?

We can have the best ideas on the planet but if our teams don't understand them, believe in them, or see how they could work in reality, then those ideas will go nowhere. So much depends on others catching our vision and being willing to follow it; without this we cannot drive change forward. Getting *buy in* from staff, young people, parents, and the wider community matters hugely because we rely on it to drive our plans forward. We have all seen the criticism, cynicism, community disintegration and resignation that can happen when there is no buy in from stakeholders. Resignation can play out in two different ways: those who do not want to buy into what you are 'selling' will either literally resign and move elsewhere if they can; or if they cannot (for personal and practical reasons), they will stay and resign themselves to paying lip service. Both forms are a problem for a leader trying to get people to connect with their vision and help them to move it forward. When it comes to buy in, you have to know what you are selling and so do other people.

WHY DO WE FIND THIS HARD?

Getting buy in is hard because it takes more time and effort than just telling people what to do. It takes consideration around *how* we will get our team on board and not just *what* we are going to do. It means we have to explain ourselves more, outline the plan in detail so that people can grasp what is being proposed, and we also have to listen to the team's thoughts and then act on them. This all takes time and perhaps that is why this is so hard. Of course, we want people to fully understand our approach and buy in to what we are doing, but time is sometimes against us, and our fear is that we will run out of runway while trying to land the plane. Getting buy in requires us to think deeply, strategically, and practically. To think of the *project* and the *people* and to bring those things together to create belief. What is really hard is that our idea will only succeed if people believe in it, and so we need to invest time in making that more likely.

If we do not get the right people onboard and with us then there will be consequences and risks for us, our teams, and our schools.

WITHOUT BUY IN ...

1: CULTURAL SABOTEURS CAN RISE UP

In *The Barcelona Way*, Damian Hughes talks about 'cultural assassins' and 'cultural architects' (sometimes referred to as 'drains' and 'radiators') to explain what happens when people do not buy in to the culture, the approach, or even to you as the leader. Cultural assassins start undermining (perhaps quietly and subtly) and will resist you and your plans and encourage others to do the same. Cultural architects are those who are with you, are bought in, and will help you build the culture or the plan that you want. Now of course, human beings are not simply one thing or another, we are complex creatures, and it is helpful to look for changes: has someone who was previously an 'architect' started to change and show different behaviours? Why? Has someone who was an 'assassin' started to change and believe in what you are doing? People can change their view and often they will respond positively if what we are saying, and how we are saying it, is clear, compelling, and easy to understand.

2: WE CANNOT GET TO WHERE WE WANT TO BE

In *Good to Great*, Jim Collins talks about having the right people on the bus first *before* we know where we are going. This was a pattern his research identified in 'good' companies that ended up being and staying great. Collins showed that to create buy in and real change, we must have disciplined people, disciplined thought, and disciplined action. He talks about 'first who, then what'. When we identify the who, especially in senior teams, we need to know that we all want the same thing, and we are comfortable in expressing the different ideas we have about how we get there. Buy in is a lot to do with the people, not just the plans.

3: PEOPLE WILL MAKE UP THEIR OWN NARRATIVE

This is not unusual in schools where staff, parents, and young people are not bought in. If we introduce something and people do not understand the what, why, or how, then they will start to make up their own narrative. For example, if you have recently launched a new cold calling policy around asking questions in classrooms but have not effectively communicated why you are doing it, how you will do it, its benefits, and the specifics of how to make it work then there may be misunderstandings. A young person may go home and say, 'we are not allowed to speak in the class anymore', or 'putting our hands up has been banned', or worse 'the teacher keeps picking on me even if I haven't got my hand up and don't know the answer'. If we leave the narrative to small children or teenagers, of course we risk it being the wrong one and the opportunity for buy in will be lost. We can't always avoid negative narratives emerging, but being on the front foot and ensuring that the right narrative is being told explicitly is helpful to avoid these incidents and encourage buy in. A Teacher Tapp survey in December 2023 stated that the main thing that staff in schools wanted from their Senior Leadership Teams (SLT) was better communication – people don't want to make up their own narrative, they would much rather be bought in to yours.

4: WE BECOME LESS BRAVE

Alignment around the *why* is great, but that isn't usually the problem in schools. The issue is often the *what* and the *how*, which must also both be clear to the team. If we know what we are aiming for, and the team understands and believes in it, then we all feel more courageous to try new things in pursuit of the aim. If this understanding does not exist, you will constantly feel that you cannot make changes or move things forward because people won't come with you. If you feel like this, then you start to feel paralysed. That is never good for you or your leadership.

MAKING IT HAPPEN – PRACTICAL IDEAS AND TOOLS

We need to know some practical ways of getting buy in and this may well be something that you have never had a 'training session' on in your career to date. Here are some practical things to try.

1: SOCIALISE THE IDEA – DEMONSTRATE THAT YOU LISTEN AND RESPOND

Buy in to making a change or trying something new often doesn't happen without some significant preparation. Very few leaders can suggest a massive change without anyone knowing anything about it before the announcement. When we are planning a change that requires buy in, we need to socialise the idea and allow it to iterate as we talk. This stage can take weeks or months, but the more the ideas are socialised, the better. This may mean you gather different teams together and talk the planned changes through – this may include parents, young people or other leaders in other schools who bring their wisdom. Give the idea a good airing, over a period of time and not only will your final proposal improve but more people will believe in it too. Where leaders fail to do this, there isn't buy in, but rather, fall out. Socialising ideas with students, parents and staff can often be helpful for you to see the early response.

2: ENSURE EVERYTHING YOU LAUNCH MAKES THE *WHY*, THE *WHAT*, AND THE *HOW* CLEAR

When we only give headlines, there are different reactions. Those people who like the big picture and are comfortable with high levels of uncertainty will not be too concerned that the details behind the headline are not there (for now). However, those people who know that what you are saying will fall to them to implement (but have no detail or instruction) will need more than good intentions and a big picture direction to feel confident to buy in. It may not be your job as the leader to go from the big picture into the detail, but it must be done. We must not underestimate the panic and anxiety it can create in parts of our team when they do not know how something is going to work. For everything we do that requires a change we should be clear about:

a. *Why* is this an issue: 'The issue we are wanting to address is ... and it needs addressing because ...'

b. *What* are we going to do: 'What we are proposing to address this is ...'

c. *How* are we going to do it: 'You will see that we have provided … to help you implement … The role of your team is …'

3: COMMUNICATE THAT YOU UNDERSTAND THE LIMITS OF THE PLAN

Nothing leads to 'opt out' quicker than when a plan is presented with obvious flaws which are not discussed or planned for. The first thing most people think when they are presented with a new idea or approach is, 'How is that going to work?' We must have answers to that question. I find it is nearly always best to be upfront about any limits in either logistics or impact. We need to be honest enough to say, 'We know that this plan may impact on the use of the dining hall and so …', or 'We know that there are some risks with this approach, and we have identified those as …'. Next, we must outline what we are going to do to ensure that these issues are overcome as well as possible. Sometimes, we are quick to act and slow to think – with change it is best to be the other way round. We must spend longer thinking through our plans before we launch, or we will spend too much time trying to fix what has gone wrong because it wasn't thought through properly. Buy in often comes when people can see that a plan has been well thought through.

4: KEEP YOUR PROMISES

Buy in can be hard to gain but quick to lose. People need to trust that when you say you will do something, you will do it. When it comes to parents and staff, being people of our word often quickly wins buy in. Conversely, buy in is often lost over fairly minor things, and then becomes very hard to regain for the major things. This is particularly important where there are strained relationships. If we are trying to get buy in from parents, spend time listening to what they have to say, try to understand how communication will best work (letter, call, or WhatsApp group, etc.), and, crucially, when you make promises, write them down on a simple spreadsheet and record when each is delivered. This helps in two main ways: firstly, it ensures that you are not overpromising and under-delivering; and, secondly, it creates a log where both parties can see that there has been action taken and promises kept. This builds trust and buy in.

5: SPEAK TO THOSE WHO HAVE NOT BOUGHT IN

Most people are not trying to be difficult; they feel under pressure because they don't understand. The fastest way to lose buy in and trust is by shutting these people down without hearing their concerns. We *must* let them express their disquiet, ask them 'What are your concerns?', 'Will this work?', 'What is missing?' Try to keep these meetings productive rather than moan fests but we *do* need to listen; sceptics may just see a major flaw in your plan that will make the whole thing come crashing down and mean we lose our credibility in the process. These people can stop us being too reactive and can help bring nuance to something we may think is very simple (but isn't!). If you listen, respond, change/tweak then these people can become your greatest assets because they will then be bought in. You are not asking for buy in without questioning (I hope) but *how* that questioning happens is important, and what you do with those questions is even more so. Questioning a plan and the implementation of it is not sabotage or being a cultural assassin, it is good team behaviour.

If you have gone through all of these steps – socialised the idea, listened to those who don't agree, and made changes or adjustments – and *then* someone deliberately attempts to undermine (and tries to take other people with them), then that is clearly a very different situation. That would need to be addressed in a different way.

> **Head Space: Thinking about your team**
> 1. What are the big things happening now that you need buy in from your team to make work?
> 2. How do you socialise your ideas? What does this look like for you?
> 3. Who in your team has not bought in right now? Why?
> 4. How easy is it for your team to challenge and question your plans? What evidence do you have that they will do this?

CHAPTER 2:
HOW TO GALVANISE A TEAM AND KEEP MOMENTUM GOING

WHY DOES THIS MATTER?

Even once you have that initial buy in from people the job is not over, far from it. If you have great ideas and have launched them effectively and got your team to buy into them (see last chapter), then there ought to be some excitement about the coming change. However, even with this good start, excitement before a change is fragile and never more so than just before and after launch. If we fail to keep momentum or galvanise our teams, then ultimately we won't achieve what we set out to.

Early in a project, there is nearly always an implementation dip when we, or our teams, may start to wonder if these plans were a good idea or if they will work at all. This is when we need to be able to galvanise the team, work through the teething issues, and keep people with us. This really matters because if we have people who are not engaging, not following through, and not convinced that things will ever turn, then they can lose belief and just stop. If too many people do that, your plans will fail. Keeping people engaged and able to maintain momentum is something that needs a lot more planning that we give it credit for.

WHY DO WE FIND THIS HARD?

Trying to keep people engaged immediately after implementation is hard. Sometimes we make it even harder for ourselves because:

- We didn't get the buy in the first place so now we are in the delicate territory when things start going wrong and people start opting out.
- We haven't thought through the unintended consequences and now we are surrounded by them.
- We haven't planned an 'exit' if our plan really isn't working and so addressing problems then feel high stakes and responsive.
- It all made perfect sense to us and so we don't understand why it doesn't to others too.
- We have moved on to the next thing and so the last thing slowly dies.

The problem with all of this of course, is that it feels chaotic to the people on the ground who are having to implement our plans. There are too many plans, too many implications, and too much being asked of staff, and all of these demands may not be clear. We need to galvanise people to keep going when it gets hard and keep the momentum going. These two things are linked.

WHAT DO WE MEAN BY 'GALVANISING' A TEAM?

The Britannica Dictionary defines galvanise as, 'to cause (people) to become so excited or concerned about an issue, idea, etc. that they want to do something about it'. If we are *not* feeling galvanised then we can become de-motivated, bored, critical, and lose our mojo. If we feel like that then a number of things are at risk: our mental fitness, our ability to cope, our energy and drive, and our sense of satisfaction.

Author and executive coach Marshall Goldsmith, in his book *Mojo*, writes about the difference between 'mojo' and 'nojo'. He defines 'mojo' as when we have a joy within that radiates outwards and 'nojo' as an aura that projects similarly but embodies 'no joy'. In chapter 1 we looked at radiators and drains – cultural architects and cultural assassins – but it could be that underlying all of those behaviours is whether a person has mojo or nojo. Goldsmith describes what happens to our behaviour when we have mojo vs when we don't.

When we have 'mojo':

- We want to take responsibility.
- We can see how to move forward.
- We go the extra mile.
- We love doing what we are doing.
- We appreciate opportunities.
- We are happy to make the best of the situation.
- We feel inspirational.
- We have a zest for life.
- We feel 'awake'.

When we have 'nojo':

- We can play the victim.
- We stick to our place and follow instructions.
- We are satisfied with the bare minimum.
- There is a feeling of obligation that we have to do something.
- We will tolerate what is being required of us.
- We start just enduring things.
- We can be painful to be around.
- We become resentful.
- We are uninterested.
- We feel indifferent.
- Inside, we feel 'zombie-like'.
- We feel 'asleep'.

If someone is feeling galvanised then they feel very excited, afraid, or angry, and these are three quite different emotions. When we launch something, it is likely that our motivation in doing so was enthusiasm about the possibilities it offers, fear, or anger. For example, we may be excited about new the opportunities we can offer staff and young people, or a new approach, or new ideas. We may be afraid of results dropping; an inspection result, retention and recruitment issues, or falling roles. We may be driven by anger about injustice, inequality, or poverty, and that can spur us on and galvanise us to make change.

To galvanise other people, we must listen to what they are saying and know where they are at. We have to 'read the room'. When people are galvanised and excited, they may say things such as:

- 'I can do this.'
- 'I see the vision.'
- 'I can contribute.'
- 'I can make a difference.'
- 'This is possible.'
- 'We can do great things.'

When they are galvanized from a place of being afraid, they may say things like:

- 'We don't want X to happen and so I am going to work with you to do Y.'
- 'We've got limited time so let's act.'
- 'There are consequences if we don't do X and they are scarier than Y.'
- 'We have to act because if we don't …'
- 'This can't fail because X is at risk.'

If people are galvanized by anger, then they may say things like:

- 'We see injustice and we cannot ignore it.'
- 'We must respond.'
- 'We will show them.'
- 'I have had enough.'
- 'This isn't right, we have to do something!'
- 'Just watch me … I will show them.'

There are many examples in the last few years, when the education sector has been galvanized from one of these positions of excitement, fear, or anger: Ofsted reform, RAAC in schools, curriculum redesign, looking after our school communities in Covid lockdowns. I shall leave you to decide which emotions were at play in each of these examples!

When people feel these things, they get determined, get righteously angry, get motivated, feel adrenaline, have purpose, and step up. They also get creative and active, they start planning, they feel energized, and they want to move things forward. When a team feels like this the energy creates the momentum that drives change. Those teams are a joy to lead and be part of and they create bonds that often last well beyond the time those people share in a school.

MAKING IT HAPPEN – PRACTICAL IDEAS AND TOOLS

How do we create this type of energy in our teams? There are a number of practical things we can do when we realise that our teams are beginning to lose momentum and need to be galvanised. Nearly all of them are simple and do not take much time, but they do require us to be aware enough to spot the signs of waning energy!

1. BE AWARE OF ENERGY LEVELS AND BE OPEN TO ASKING YOUR TEAM ABOUT THEM

At the start of meetings, ask people, 'How are your energy levels?', it may change how the meeting then plays out. If energy levels are low, we can agree on the best way to conduct the meeting. It may be that some decisions are not made as people are not in the right mindset to be objective. It may mean that we do short and sharp updates, include more discussion, or change the meeting entirely. If people's energy levels are low, it is often because they are feeling or experiencing something you may not even know about. Ask them what they need.

Trying to lift the energy in the room can be done by asking people to tell each other the funniest thing they have experienced this week, recount a moment when they laughed, or why they came into the job – this only takes three minutes but watch the energy levels rise. Or the team may just need a drink, or five minutes of silence at the start of the meeting while they all write down everything that they are carrying in their head on paper, and then they will be able to fully concentrate.

2. REINFORCE THE VISION

This can be done in a number of ways:

a. Bring out a press release that you have written from the point of view of the future, reminding people of where you are heading.

b. Choose one young person/teacher who you know has benefited from what you have put in place and tell their story.

   c. Choose a young person/teacher who has not seen impact yet, but you know will if what you are doing works and tell that story.

   d. Read out some positive emails/letters that provide evidence that things are improving.

   e. Look back on where you were and identify the key changes that made the progress from that point possible.

   f. Reflect on the qualities the team is showing to pull things off.

   g. Ask the team what they hope their legacy will be.

3. KNOW WHAT GALVANISES DIFFERENT MEMBERS OF THE TEAM

Patrick Lencioni talks about the way teams work when individuals have different talents and preferences. In his book, *The 6 Types of Working Genius* he outlines six qualities:

   a. Wonder.

   b. Invention.

   c. Discernment.

   d. Galvanising.

   e. Enablement.

   f. Tenacity.

Some people are really good at galvanising others, and can get people energised, engaged, and ready to take action. Other people are not good at this skill, and we should not assume that everyone has this gift. All leaders need this skill but not everyone finds it easy. Those of us who *do* like galvanising also need to be aware that people respond to different things. Someone with the gift of tenacity will perhaps be inspired by your words but ultimately, they will want to take practical actions and we must enable them to be able to do that. Those who have the gift of wonder or invention are needed – and can inspire others – but if they head off in their excitement without thinking through the possible unintended consequences or logistics on the ground, the result could be a team who are not galvanised at all! If you have someone who can galvanise people then they will be an important part of the team, but only if they are galvanising people to attempt things which can actually happen in reality!

4. CELEBRATE THE SPECIAL OCCASIONS AND LANDMARKS AND SHOW GRATITUDE

Once we have a plan set up and start to see things turning around it is easy to skate over progress, but recognising milestones is important. These things may well be small: the first time you have 100% attendance at an after-school club; the moment a year group has an improved average reading age; doing a silent fire drill in record time; or when you have improved in a national measure that has been a struggle for you. We need to make a list of things we will celebrate on the way to where we are heading. These things may not be the ultimate change we want to achieve but they are significant indicators that we are on the right road.

When we celebrate these things, we need to recognise the team's hard work and show gratitude in ways that will not cost a fortune but will help to galvanise the team. These things should be small, unexpected, above the ordinary, and crucially *valued*, like providing fresh milk, biscuits or catering before an event. Some schools operate a Guardian Angel system where staff are secretly paired up and do a series of nice things for each other over a particularly hard term; this can be buying chocolate bars, leaving positive praise on a postcard on the desk, or simply bringing a cup of tea ... These things don't cost a lot in the grand scheme of things but when things are difficult and energy is waning, they can really help!

5. SPEND TIME ENGAGING WITH BOTH STAFF AND STUDENTS

Whether it is walking the corridors and speaking to young people, or going into the nurture room, sometimes we all need to get out of the office or meeting and see people to be re-galvanised. Invest in 1:1 meetings to help galvanise others. Talk with some students about how things are going with them. See that your vision *is* the reality.

6. ALLOW PEOPLE TO LOOK BEYOND THE SCHOOL GATES

Visiting schools can work in two ways, if people go to another school and can see that you are doing similar things then this can build confidence and re-energise them and their colleagues when they return. If they go to another school and see that you are further on in some areas in your journey than the other school, that can bring them feelings of gratitude and encouragement. All of us benefit from seeing the grass on the other side of the fence to renew our perspective.

Head Space: Thinking about your team

1. Think of a recent situation where you felt galvanized into action:
   - What was the emotion that you felt? Was it excitement, fear, or anger?
   - What was your reaction and what did you pledge to do?
2. Where is there currently diminishing momentum in your team? What is the reason for this and what might you do to try and galvanise them again?
3. It may be that you are not a natural galvaniser. Who is the best 'galvaniser' in your team? How often are they using that skill?

CHAPTER 3:
HOW TO HAVE MEANINGFUL MEETINGS

We have a lot of meetings in school life: parents' meetings and evenings, department/team meetings, SLT meetings, governor's meetings, and of course all the meetings that happen as part of continued professional development. On top of that we have meetings with outside agencies and other stakeholders. We run meetings and we will be in them. Meetings take hours of our time and so it really does matter how they are planned, run, and managed. Great meetings can energise, inspire, and make a call to action. Bad meetings can leave people feeling like they have wasted both time and energy. When people are lacking both of these commodities, using them wisely is particularly important.

Running meaningful meetings is hard work. Cancelling pointless meetings takes courage. Planning meetings so that they are purposeful and productive is crucial. We do not want the people we work with to feel that 'a meeting is an event where minutes are taken and hours wasted', as the old wisecrack goes.

WHY DO WE FIND THIS HARD?

There are many reasons why running effective meetings is hard, particularly when we are busy and time constrained (or distracted by events happening in school). It takes a lot of thought, and consequently most of us simply default to running them in the same way that we always have. Some common issues with meetings are:

- They have the wrong people in them.
- We don't always know what they are for or how they will work.
- We have either too little or too much time.
- Some meetings should have been an email or a briefing!
- Some emails *should* have been a meeting!

It is unlikely that you have ever had any training on 'how to run meetings', it doesn't tend to be on many of the courses I have seen. Yet it is an essential part of being a leader. How can we run highly effective meetings that leave people in a better place than when they came in?

MAKING IT HAPPEN – PRACTICAL IDEAS AND TOOLS

1. GET THE RIGHT PEOPLE IN THE MEETING

Sometimes we plan a strategy during a meeting but the people who have to deliver what we have planned are not there. If they had been, they would have pointed out that some of what we asked for has logistical limits or unintended consequences. In general, we tend not to have meetings across the school structure – with all the different levels affected by a change or strategy represented – and as a result we lose a lot of valuable intelligence.

It is helpful to look at what you are trying to achieve and then ask, 'who would be helpful to have in this meeting and who doesn't need to be there?' For example, if you are the pastoral deputy head in an all through school, and you are planning to run a silent fire drill practice for the first time, then it may be helpful to have a meeting with the key people involved first. You could, of course, just send an email but for people to really buy into what you are doing and to understand how to make this happen, it will be helpful to hear from people across the school. For example:

CHAPTER 3: HOW TO HAVE MEANINGFUL MEETINGS

- Early years lead – what do they need? How much warning should there be? What is the best timing for the practice so that they haven't got to help put on 60 pairs of shoes and coats at speed?!
- Year 11 pastoral – are there any exams/mocks planned which would cause issues?
- Catering lead – check the timing of leaving the building so food isn't wasted.
- Site manager – is the site secure?
- Office team – are they ready with everything they need to take the register.

Other people bring different perspectives. If you are having a meeting about what motivates sixth form students, then it may be helpful to invite a couple along to speak. If you are about to introduce a new system for middle leaders, then it is helpful to socialise the idea with some of them. You need be clear about the purpose of inviting them, but they will very often tell you a view that you haven't thought about. True leadership is listening to these views and mixing people up, Amy Edmondson calls this 'extreme teaming' (for a set time, for a set purpose, and with a wider range of people).

2. ALWAYS KNOW THE PURPOSE OF THE MEETING

Sometimes we have a meeting simply because it is in the calendar, but even if we have an agenda, we are sometimes not clear what it is for: a decision, discussion, information only, or pre-warning of something coming in the future. As a result, we don't always allocate the right amount of time to each item or don't have all the relevant information required to make an informed decision. This in turn means that we don't always make the best decisions or know what is expected of the people in the team.

You will have sat in meetings and not been sure if you are meant to say anything: whether this is the time to raise concerns, or whether it is a done deal. Much of the time is then spent wondering what part you are meant to play. Think about the last meeting you were in:

- Did you know what it was for?
- Did you know what your role was? For example, were you meant contribute, give your opinion, or just listen. Was this meeting

meant to identify disagreement and to mine for conflict, or was it to rubber stamp decisions?

- Did you know how to put forward a challenge if needed? Did others in the room who are less experienced than you know how to raise a challenge?

- Did you know what you were meant to have achieved by the end?

- If the meeting over ran over and someone had to leave to pick up their children, would that have been acceptable?

When constructing meeting agendas, outline the overall purpose of the meeting (e.g. to plan the calendar for next year) and then itemise each item with a clear direction and time. Where there is pre-reading, specify this too and ensure it is available in good time. Do not allow reading to be added at the last minute, as this will then not be read by everyone. Pre-reading helps to align people without wasting meeting time getting everyone up to speed. For example:

- Parents' evening pattern: *Info only*, 5 mins.
- Open days: *Discussion* 30 mins (pre-reading available).
- Training days next year: *Decision* 20 mins.

These simple steps help to manage expectations so that people can concentrate on what they are saying, not whether they should be saying it.

3. COMMUNICATE WITH THE TEAM IN THE CORRECT FORMAT

Unnecessary meetings are not a good use of time. If things can be sent in an email, then sometimes that is best. However, sometimes even things that *could* be communicated via email *do* need to be meetings so that people can hear the tone and sentiment behind what is being said. Making the call on what needs to be in an email and what should be in a meeting requires leaders to understand their team and how things will land with them.

There are different ways of communicating with people to help land messages:

- An email followed by a drop-in session to find out more.
- A video sent round (with the transcript to read if people prefer).

- A briefing followed up with clear actions/logistics.
- Briefing middle leaders who then brief their departments.
- An email – if it is clear cut information.
- A meeting – if people need bringing together to hear things as a whole team.

4. AVOID LEADERSHIP TEAM 'MEETING SOUP'

Sometimes we pack an agenda so full that we are defeated before we even start. This means that some agenda items are under-cooked, while others are overdone, and it can lead to going faster and faster but with less and less clarity. By the end of the meeting people are exhausted and we are in danger of overrunning, which means we then don't record the actions. It would have been better to have less on the agenda and allow more time. This approach is like 'meeting soup', everything is blended into one type of meeting at the same time. A meeting will inevitably lose its individual flavour and sharpness when everything is thrown in.

Lencioni' s *Death by Meeting* suggests the following four types of meetings. As a leadership team, which of these do you already do?

Meeting Type	Time	Purpose and Format	Top Tips
Daily Check In	5 mins	What is happening today? Anyone to be aware of? Who is where? Duty rotas. Students on the list to positively engage with.	Standing up. Don't cancel. Focused on today and administration. Needs discipline with time and structure.
Weekly Tactical	45-90 mins	Review the week/targets/lead measures. Resolve immediate issues. Team creates the agenda to ensure things are addressed. Remove obstacles and address challenges.	Ask people to contribute agenda items. Avoid lengthy strategic decisions. Reinforce clarity and update pre-mortems.

Monthly strategic leadership meeting (or ad hoc strategic)	2-4 hours	Discuss. Analyse. Work through big issues impacting progress/results/success. Re-visit, pre-mortem, and look ahead.	Limit to 1 or 2 important topics so you can go deeper. Research and preparation required. Pre-reading helpful. Encourage productive conflict and disagreement.
Termly off site Review	1 day	Review the strategy. Review impact. How is the team? Anything we need to change?	Get out of school. Allow discussions to happen. Don't overly structure the time.

5. CREATE THE RIGHT TYPE OF DRAMA

Lencioni believes that if meetings lack the right type of drama, then we do not get the best out of the people in them. He suggests there are three things that we can do in meetings to create this drama:

- **The hook** – at the start of the meeting, the leader talks about the dangers of making a bad decision or a wrong judgement, or highlights something that may cause a threat or concern. If this is made clear within the first ten minutes, then everyone is jolted into action and focused thought.

- **Mine for conflict** – if the disagreement doesn't come out here, then it will come out somewhere else and cause frustration. The leader should look for the issues where there are disagreements over approach and ensure that there is time and space to explore them properly and disagree openly. It is better to discuss disagreements openly than through corridor conversations in private. Lencioni argues, 'the only thing more painful than confronting an uncomfortable topic is pretending it doesn't exist'. Whispered conversations privately can cause damage to both your team and plans.

- **Real time permission** – give permission for people to express critical or negative thoughts, play devil's advocate, or to be the downer and challenge the excitement. Going round the room and asking, 'what are your concerns?' is better than asking, 'any concerns?' The former assumes that they will have concerns, the latter does not. One gives the permission to open up, the other closes it down.

6. ENABLE PEOPLE TO BE THE BEST VERSION OF THEMSELVES

Meetings in schools often happen after a full day of working with young people. Many people find themselves on the fly from teaching, to gate duty, to your meeting. It is unlikely that people will be at their best immediately but there are some very simple and obvious things we can do to help. You may already know these strategies, but the key is actually using them:

- Tea, coffee, water, and biscuits provided for people as standard (with a clean mug!).

- Give people five minutes at the start of the meeting to empty their whirring thoughts on to a post-it note or to do list. This is best done in silence while people gather their thoughts. People are more focused when they are not distracted.

- Start with a leadership reflection that gets people out of one mindset into another one. Things like: 'Time is precious, we don't waste it'.

A way of understanding the 'cost' of meetings is to roughly calculate how much this meeting is costing you as a group. Work this out by roughly working out your hourly rates and adding them together. Give this meeting a 'cost'. A good question to ask is, 'what are the benefits of meeting together like this, what does it help us achieve?'

7. ENSURE CLARITY AT THE END OF EVERY MEETING

Leave ten minutes at the end to note down key actions, with initials and timeframes, and decisions made as to the most important for the team to action. Recap these elements at the end of the meeting to ensure that everyone is in agreement. Rather than have emails flying around, having one central area on a shared drive that tracks actions (which people can access themselves to mark their actions as done) helps keep things on track.

NINE LEVELS OF DELEGATION

Another way of gaining clarity is by using the nine levels of delegation, designed by Tim Brighouse and David Woods, to help everyone understand and agree on what they own and what they don't. It is important to know what you, as the leader, want in terms of information vs decisions vs actions. In some contexts, you will be a number one and in other things, a number eight. Make that clear to people and explain why:

1. Look into this problem. Give me all the facts. I will decide what to do.

2. Let me know the options available, with the pros and cons of each. I will decide what to select.

3. Let me know the criteria for your recommendation, which alternatives you have identified, and which one appears best to you, with any risks identified. I will make the decision.

4. Recommend a course of action for my approval.

5. Let me know what you intend to do. Delay action until I approve.

6. Let me know what you intend to do. Do it unless I say not to.

7. Take action. Let me know what you did. Let me know how it turns out.

8. Take action. Communicate with me only if the action is unsuccessful.

9. Take action. No further communication with me is necessary.

> **Head Space: Thinking about your team**
>
> 1. How comfortable do you feel in allowing constructive conflict and disagreement?
>
> 2. If people in your team knew what was expected of them and were given permission to raise challenges, how would it change your meetings?
>
> 3. What would be the benefit for your team of the four types of meeting model? Draft out what you would cover in each format if you were to hold them, and how it would move your team forward.
>
> 4. How would using the Brighouse and Woods nine levels model help people be clearer about what it is you want?

CHAPTER 4:
HOW TO OVERCOME DYSFUNCTION IN THE TEAM

When teams are not working well (for whatever reason) it can be a very difficult issue to try and solve. When teams are dysfunctional, communication suffers, buy in wanes, momentum stutters, and people get critical, defensive, frustrated, and demotivated. When this happens, we are not able to make strides forwards because all of us are on high alert, or we might feel like we have to learn not to care so that we can manage day-to-day. This damages the team, stops progress happening and creates a working environment that people start to dread. Dysfunction can occur in different areas: relationships, communication, direction, or implementation, to name a few. Working through dysfunction and understanding why it is happening and what we can do about it is something that all leaders need to have in their toolkit. When we are struggling with the complexity of the situation, we need models that can help us see clearly what is happening, that help us manage complex change, and help us get the best out of people once again.

WHY DO WE FIND THIS HARD?

Experiencing team dysfunction is hard! If we are the leaders of a dysfunctional team, we often feel hopeless because although we know there is a problem, we don't really know the root cause, or how to solve it. We often don't know where to start or how to call out the elephant in the room. We might think it is just us, or that it is our fault, and so often we are working through our own feelings as well as those of the team. Even when we *do* know what the problem is – and we know that we have to address it – we sometimes delay because it is awkward or because we don't feel we have the tools to be able to handle the situation well. As a result, sometimes we continue in the dysfunction for some time until it comes to a head. However, while dysfunction persists, it not only impacts us personally, but it affects the team, their work, and how happy people feel. If you have ever been in a dysfunctional team, you will know that it is not an enjoyable experience. There is very little laughter because people don't feel safe enough to laugh (see more in chapter 6: how to be safe and brave).

MAKING IT HAPPEN – PRACTICAL IDEAS AND TOOLS.

1. LOOK INTO HOW ALL TEAMS WORK, NOT JUST THE SLT

In his book *Nine Lies About Work*, Marcus Buckingham identifies lie number one as 'people care which company they work for'. His research is from the world of business, but the findings are important to consider in schools too and might be as shocking to us in education as it was to businesses. Buckingham's research suggests that the local experiences that people have in teams within an organisation are what dictates whether they will stay or go, thrive, or merely survive. Buckingham states that, 'while people might care which company they join, they don't care which company they work for. The truth is that, once there, *people care which team they're on*'. If this is true, then we ought to make sure that *every* team in school is operating well. We need to find the best teams and ensure that every other team is reaching the same level. If we don't, we will find, that despite your brilliant leadership and your high performing SLT, you can't keep staff in other teams because things there are not working as well.

Teams matter, Buckingham argues, because they simplify, they make the work real, and they make homes for individuals. It is in localised teams that we can unlock brilliance, embrace uniqueness, and ensure that individual contributions add up to a greater collective effort. Do we know if this is what is *really* happening in all of our teams?

2. ASK YOURSELF HONEST QUESTIONS

We can reflect on our own leadership, but we also need to reflect on our team dynamics. Is it clear how well you are working as a team? Have you defined how you want the team to function? Imagine that you are taking the position of a bystander watching as your team meets, what do you see? It is helpful to run that narrative while commenting on yourself in the third person:

- What is happening? '[name] opens the meeting and is clear about the purpose of the meeting. He doesn't notice that three people are on their phones, and one is emailing. People seem distracted.'

- What are the dynamics? '[name] dominates the conversation and shuts people down when they speak' or '[name] appears defensive and doesn't contribute as much as others' or 'there is high quality and robust discussion in the group and energy levels are high.'

- If you could pause the action and change one thing, what would it be?

Now, look at these questions and answer red (R) if this is not currently true, amber (A) if this is sometimes true, or green (G) this if is always true next to each statement. Try this yourself and then, if you are a little braver, ask your team members to also fill in the table to help you get a collective view of the team.

Team statement	How true is this? R/A/G
We are a dynamic team of individuals.	
We share the same values.	
We are able to adapt to new ways of working.	
We provide high support and high challenge to each other.	
We foster a culture where we feel safe and brave together.	
We are deliberate about inspiring change.	
We help each other feel valued, loved, encouraged, and equipped.	
We recognise opportunities within the challenges of the job.	
We 'tag out' when something isn't working.	
We trust each other's judgement.	
When things go wrong, we do not seek to blame others.	
We want to be part of this team.	
We actively pursue ways to make our team stronger.	
We understand the importance of team development.	
We create a culture that is unmissable.	
We actively pursue audacious ideas.	
We manage our emotions and are able to stay 'present' with each other.	

3. ASK YOURSELF, IS SOMETHING MISSING FROM YOUR TEAM?

The Lippitt-Knoster model created by Mary Lippitt and Timothy Knoster, helps us see what might be missing and what happens as a result. There are five things that a team needs in order to deliver results:

- **Vision** – must be compelling and clear, shared, and constantly re-visited. The end point that we are trying to get to must be understood by everyone.

- **Consensus** – we must all agree and commit to what we are trying to achieve.

- **Skills** – we need to give people the best chance of success by ensuring they have the right competencies and skills to do the job. We often promote great teachers to leadership positions with not a hint of training on things like spreadsheets, results analysis, and coaching and then expect them to be competent in all three.

- **Incentives** – people need to feel motivated and rewarded, seen, and heard. Incentives can come in pay or promotion (although these can be limited in education!) but don't need to be either (see chapter 2).

- **Resources** – we need to ensure that our teams have sufficient resources: time, money, technology, people, and support so that they can make change happen. Without resources plans often fail. Understanding what is needed to make a difference and then finding the funding is often cited by school leaders and teachers as one of their biggest challenges.

- **Action plan** – we need to know the steps to achieving the vision. These steps must be specific, measurable, achievable, relevant, and time-bound (SMART) and clear to all involved. The very first step needs to be clear.

When all six things are in place then we are more likely to get results. However, when these things are not in place, we will get dysfunctional behaviours and challenges. When even just one thing is missing, look at what happens: confusion, sabotage, anxiety, resistance, frustration, and false starts. All are surely the very definition of a dysfunctional team! The Lippitt-Knoster model is a helpful way to identify what is missing in your teams.

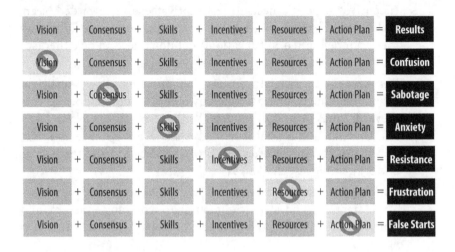

Figure 1: The Lippitt-Knoster Model

4. IDENTIFY HOW WELL YOUR TEAM IS FUNCTIONING

Another lens through which we can look at our teams is the five Dysfunctions of a Team model by Patrick Lencioni. This describes five dysfunctions in teams, all of which can be overcome and addressed but first need to be identified.

Figure 2: Lencioni's Five Dysfunctions Model

Lencioni's five team dysfunctions are:

- **Absence of trust** – This is when we are not able to feel safe or be brave because we do not trust that people are working together with the right motives or behaviours. People are not comfortable with each other and will not admit weaknesses and mistakes. Amy Edmondson calls this a lack of 'psychological safety' and we will explore this further in chapter 6.

- **Fear of conflict** – if we do not want conflict because we know it won't be harmonious (and may indeed get personal), we will not want to disagree. An artificial harmony is created because people dare not disagree. If this happens then bad decisions get made, things are overlooked, and challenge is not given because people are trying to keep the peace. If you are a people pleaser who is conflict avoidant, this may well be your position (see the first *Time to Think*). People will of course be criticising the team's decisions privately (just not publicly), resulting in a false environment where progress is stymied.

- **Lack of commitment** – lack of clarity and buy in means that people don't complete the things they have committed to, and decisions are not followed through to completion. This creates tension, impacts how things move forward, and results in ambiguity. The top performing stars in your team who want to make change and get things to happen, will be left disillusioned and disgruntled. If conflict cannot be aired, then it will largely go unsaid.

- **Avoidance of accountability** – if we lack trust, conflict, and commitment then we are not able to hold people accountable. Equally, people don't know what they are accountable for because of this ambiguity. This then leads to people feeling vulnerable in case they are about to be blamed for a decision that they didn't take, or one that they did that wasn't followed through. By this stage, there is no peer-to-peer accountability and people dare not call each other out.

- **Inattention to results** – this is when our own ego and status impacts the team getting results. We can start to focus on individual performance and leave everyone else to whatever they are doing. At this stage, people are putting themselves first, and the needs of the team last. Individuals are no longer working as a team at all. If no-one is focused on what the team needs to achieve then the school suffers, as do the outcomes.

5. ARE YOU IN A 'DOOM LOOP'?

In *Good to Great*, Jim Collins talks about 'doom loops' (which are the opposite of creating momentum) and this a pattern that is easy to recognise in education. Sometimes teams are dysfunctional because change is being managed poorly. The diagram below shows some of the pitfalls.

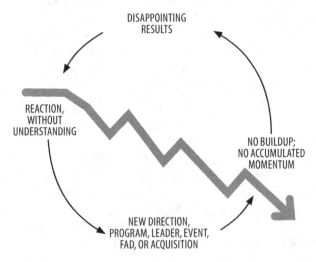

Figure 3: Doom Loops

- **Disappointing results** – this could be Ofsted inspections, outcomes, attendance, or a whole other range of things that are measured in schools. That disappointment drives us to want to change something; in itself, that desire is not wrong, but we have to be careful how we react in case we cause further dysfunction.

- **Reaction without understanding** – if we react but do not understand the root causes of what has happened then we are going to make mistakes. Understanding is key but checking that understanding is even more important. Are our assumptions correct? How do we know? Are we sure that what we are asserting can be evidenced? Have we asked a wide range of people? Is our reaction reliable or is it knee-jerk?

- **New direction, program, leader, event, fad, or acquisition** – if we are acting from disappointment and are driven by that reaction without understanding the roots of the problem then it is very likely that we are going to think that there is a simple solution. Sometimes we move staff, sometimes we appoint new ones, we may restructure, re-organise, re-design the curriculum, or something else. These things *may* even work, but without real understanding we risk making the situation worse.

- **No build-up; no accumulated momentum** – if we have chosen the wrong response, that won't make the biggest difference, then we will see a lack of build-up, buy in, and momentum, which in turn then leads to more disappointing results. Those results then start the doom loop over again.

The doom loop feels really hard when you are in it. Wherever you start on the diagram, if we are led by our reactions and a shallow understanding, we can make significant mistakes which can cause dysfunction. Nobody wants to be here. Sometimes we inherit a situation where the school or team has been in a doom loop for some time, and we need to ensure that it does not continue. On other occasions, we may be the ones who have inadvertently caused the doom loop. Either way, if we are aware of this dynamic then we will be less likely to fall into it without realising.

Head Space: Thinking about your team

1. Looking across your school, where are the examples of great teams and what is it that they do that makes them work so well?

2. Where do you think there may be dysfunction in teams? What are they and why?

3. Look at the Lippitt-Knoster Grid – what is missing in your team and what is the result of that deficiency?

4. Looking at Lencioni's five dysfunctions, which of these issues affect your team or the teams you work with?

5. Identify two issues that you need to think more about. Schedule that time in your diary to ensure it is not lost.

CHAPTER 5:
HOW TO GET INTO 'DEEP WORK'

WHY DOES THIS MATTER?

'Deep Work' is a phrase coined by researcher Cal Newport in his book of the same name. Newport states that the ability to be able to concentrate and engage in deeper work is becoming very rare at the same time as it is becoming increasingly valuable to the workplace and the economy. He goes so far as to say that those who are able to engage in deep work regularly, will thrive. The ability to concentrate and remove ourselves from all the distractions really is important because we are constantly suffering from split concentration and cognitive overload with very few chances to get into what psychologist Mihaly Csikszentmihalyi calls 'flow'.

There is a constant hum of distraction when we sit down to work, we are unable to concentrate for very long before there is a knock at the door, a radio message, a ping on a phone, or an email arrives in the inbox. All of this is eroding our ability to be distraction free. Ironically, for educational institutions, schools are not always a great place for staff to get into deep work when it comes to planning and thinking. That is why most people do their most important planning and thinking in their own time, at home. Our relationship with the important over the urgent needs to be re-visited because we are finding people at every level in schools are exhausted, frustrated, and often overwhelmed. Finding the time, in working hours, for deep work is something the education sector has to get better at. Getting deep work right is a win-win situation for our staff.

They will feel more in control and clearer about what they are doing, and the organisation will benefit. We need to look again at this issue because many people feel there is too much to do, and too little time to do it in, and this contributes towards our recruitment and retention crisis.

WHY DO WE FIND THIS HARD?

Deep work is a challenge for school leaders for many reasons: timetable restrictions, PPA time slots only lasting around an hour (and often not being blocked together), the nature of the responsive job, safeguarding concerns, constant emails, being 'on call', and the reality that between Monday and Wednesday your plans can change with little warning if Ofsted calls. Deep work sometimes feels out of our grasp because of the nature of working in schools. It is also hard because most of us are used to, and even prefer, what Newport calls 'shallow work'. He defines that as 'non-cognitively demanding, logistical-style tasks, often performed while distracted'.

Deep work is also a challenge when we have such a hyper-connected working (and personal) environment. Networking tools are constant distractions and erode our ability to focus, we are unable to concentrate for long periods of time without the draw of something on our phones or computers. A McKinsey study in 2012 found that the average worker was spending 60% of their working week on some form of electronic communication on the internet (30% of that time was reading and answering email alone). I would imagine that now this figure may even be higher. For school staff, most of this email checking has to happen after contact time has finished, leaving very little time for anything strategic.

Why not just turn it all off for an hour, put our phones in our bag, turn alerts off, and remove distractions? This may sound simple, but many of us find it very difficult. This is where we have to face an uncomfortable truth; many of us like shallow work because we get small things off the to do list and we feel productive and efficient. Many of us like the reactive nature of our jobs and almost welcome the distractions. Too many of us feel guilty if we do not respond to an email immediately, and wonder if the sender will be criticising us or doubting our work ethic if we don't show that we are always there, ready to respond.

Research shows that this addiction to connectivity is not serving us well. Professor Leslie Perlow at Harvard Business School found that the professionals she surveyed spent around 20 to 25 hours a week monitoring email *outside* working hours. The reason for this? They believed it was important to respond to any email within an hour of it reaching their inbox. Of course, some emails must be answered as soon as possible but many do not, and we need to be better at working out the difference. When we play 'whack a mole' with our emails then *they* dictate what is important. If your workflow and priorities are dictated by what is in your inbox, then the senders of those emails are in control of your time and thinking, not you. We end up being reactive and frustrated.

This is hard. I know there are competing demands on leaders. I know that the number of forms of communication is getting out of hand. However, I also know that we need to learn more respect for ourselves, our teams, our time, and our brains by maintaining some boundaries so that we can get to the really satisfying deep work that Newport talks about. If we do not do this, we will spend most of our working hours in the shallows and our holidays and weekends in deep work. There must be a better way. How can we maximise our working hours to ensure there is more of a balance between deep work and shallow work? Shallow should only be around 30% of our time, not the 90% it often currently is for many people.

MAKING IT HAPPEN – PRACTICAL IDEAS AND TOOLS

Teaching itself *is* deep work. The classroom is where many teachers find their 'flow', while they are absorbed in instructing, listening, responding, giving feedback, and building relationships. It is the work around teaching we will focus on here: marking, report writing, planning, analysing results, writing development plans, planning for a new strategy, etc. How can we make deep work more likely in school hours, outside of direct teaching time? These issues are not easy in schools due to timetable restrictions and the nature of the job; being in a school with lots of young people who often need our attention. If we see the benefit of deep work and want to make it our reality, then we need to do things differently. Some of the following ideas are for the whole school and others are aimed directly at you. School leaders must model this behaviour, however hard that is! These suggestions will give you some practical starting points.

1. LOOK AT YOUR COMMUNICATION STRATEGY

Emails in schools is a topic of hot debate but there are some helpful things to establish with your whole school team and your SLT (which may operate slightly differently to other staff). Whatever you choose to do, the expectations need to be clear. Some simple 'rules' around email use reduce uncertainty:

- If you are copied in that means the email is for info only. No reply is needed.

- The banner heading should state what the email is requiring from someone: Action, Decision, or Urgent. When scanning emails people can then see what needs their attention most. Too often we have to read every email to work out the priorities. This takes a long time and before we know it, we get lost down the email rabbit hole, the whole of our PPA time has gone, and we have done nothing we intended.

- Do you have a separate approach for urgent matters or is everything done through email? If everything is in email, then people will have to check it constantly or live in fear that they have missed something.

- Do you use out of office responses to manage expectations? What are the expected response times (they should not be 'instantly' or 'within the hour'!)? This is important and helps both staff and parents to manage their expectations.

- If you are the head, in the SLT or a CEO, are you brave enough to take some time to do 'deep work' and to set up an out of office saying that your responses to email will be limited? Many of us shudder at the thought and then wonder why we are constantly interrupted and distracted, stuck in shallow work cycles.

2. ESTABLISH A NEW CULTURE OF 'DEEP WORK' AND MAKE THIS EXPLICIT AND ACCOUNTABLE

If you want to promote distraction free deep work as something your staff should do at least a few times each week, then you need to model it yourself. When I suggest to headteachers that they may want to go in to school later so that they can work for two hours at home on a strategic document the response is often, 'I couldn't do that?'. When I push and ask why, the majority are anxious what other people will think of them. Perhaps we worry that people will think it is indulgent – or unfair because, 'it's all right for *you* to stay at home, we can't' – some even worry that staff may think they are not working hard enough.

I understand these concerns but … are we really saying that the leader of an organisation is not able to take two hours to write a document of vital importance to the school community if it means they come into school at 10.30am and not 8am? Of course, we have to make sure the school is stable and well-staffed, and the SLT are stepping up but as leaders, but we also have to be disciplined with our time and energy. The impact on the school from you getting that work done uninterrupted is worth the investment. An approach that helps is to tell colleagues, 'I am coming in at 10:30am tomorrow with a completed document on X for us to analyse'. Then go somewhere quiet, turn off all notifications and get into deep work. I can guarantee it will help you get clarity and feel more in control. Once you are modelling this, you will empower others to do the same. If the thought of this is bringing you out in a rash, can I recommend you read the first *Time to Think*, especially the chapters on people pleasing and boundaries.

3.TRY 'MONK MODE MORNINGS'

In *Deep Work*, Cal Newport recommends an approach called 'Monk Mode Mornings' – similar ideas are covered in a TED talk by Jason Fried called 'Why Work Doesn't Happen at Work' – it seems that it isn't only educationalists who struggle with this problem. The concept of Monk Mode Mornings is that you take the morning to go into deep work, distraction free, and tell people that you will be in communication after 12. This chunk of time is great for strategic thinking, creative problem solving, planning for the long term, or grappling with a big issue. As a head or a CEO think of what this approach would do to your productivity levels, both for you personally and then with your SLT. I am a believer in this approach: the book you are holding in your hands was written in Monk Mode Mornings across a number of months!

4. REMOVE DISTRACTIONS AND INTERRUPTIONS

This sounds easy and obvious but in schools, distractions are everywhere: walkie talkies, emails, Teams messages, phone calls, parents in reception, students knocking at the door or people wanting 'a quick word' (which usually isn't quick). I always find it interesting that none of these things would happen if you were conducting an interview, observing someone's lessons, or meeting visitors who have come into school. *Those* things have clear 'do not interrupt' boundaries, and all device beeps and peeps will have been turned off. Yet when we are sitting in the corner of the office working in PPA time, or after school, and people can see us, pretty much everyone thinks we are open to interruption. I have seen all kinds of approaches to this problem in schools: a quiet staff working room where no-one is talking, people in offices with signs on the doors saying 'meeting/webinar in progress: do not disturb' (even though they are in there working alone). I have even seen someone who put noise cancelling headphones on and stuck a A4 sign on their seat saying, 'do not talk to me, I am on a deadline!'.

For some people, working immediately after school *in* school is too hard because distractions exist everywhere. For them, leaving promptly to head somewhere else to get a couple of hours done is the best and most productive use of their time. In a world that is embracing 'flexible working' in a way that schools often can't, we could at least encourage people to find the best way of working distraction free and then enabling them to do it. Without judgement.

5. IDENTIFY THE RIGHT AMOUNT OF TIME TO GET INTO 'DEEP WORK'

Whether you are working in school or out, in your own time or in work time, giving yourself the best chance of being able to do deep work requires discipline to reap the rewards. What you produce will likely be of better quality and you will leave that time feeling great. There are clear rewards of having the time to get into 'flow'. The psychologist Mihaly Csikszentmihalyi talks about 'flow states' when we are:

• Engaged in challenging activities.
• Free from distraction.
• Engrossed in what we are doing.

- Thinking deeply and our mind is reaching full capacity.
- Doing work where the challenge and the skill level match (if we are working on something we can't do, we often find it harder to get into a flow state).

The benefits of this are clear in the research, if we are in 'flow' we feel motivated, fulfilled, efficient, productive and, as a result, generally happier. The challenge of course is finding and making the time for this to happen. In her book *Happier Hour*, Cassie Holmes writes about the optimum time for what she calls 'discretionary activity'; when we are doing something we want to do. Although her research focuses on leisure time, the principles are helpful to consider in work too. She shows that for those who feel time poor, less than two hours of discretionary activity is usually not enough and is associated with less happiness because of stress. However, more than approximately five hours a day is too much, and is also associated with less happiness, because it fosters a lack of urgency and purpose. Making sure we know the amount of deep work time that is right for us is helpful. For me, it's three hours. If I have a three-hour chunk of time set aside, I feel like I can change the world. Cal Newport's research suggests: 'the typical work day is eight hours, the most adept thinker cannot spend more than four of these hours in a state of true depth'. Finding out how you – and your team – work, will help move things forward.

6. KNOW YOU ARE WINNING

Most of us are better at strategizing than executing. The changes that I am talking about here will not happen without accountability, deliberate execution, and consciously feeling the benefit. *The 4 Disciplines of Execution*, by Covey, McChesney, and Huling promotes the use of lead measures (small, measurable actions) and compelling scoreboards (tracking on a simple chart to check if you have done what you said you would do). One lead measure might be, 'to complete a three-hour block "deep work" once a week'. Then, each week, you tick off whether you have done it or not. This system will help you schedule your time better and justify why you are making changes to your working patterns. It will keep you accountable and focused. When we can see that we are managing to implement these changes, we know that we are winning, and our timetable and diary are evidence of this. This helps build something like deep work into a habit, not a luxury!

7.LEGITIMISE WALKING AWAY FROM THE COMPUTER

Whenever you *do* find the time to do the work that needs to happen outside of contact time, it is highly unlikely that your ideas will start flowing while staring at a laptop. Thinking about an issue usually happens when we give our minds space without the threat of a blank page. It can happen at very different times – and often very inconvenient ones at that (in the middle of the night, while on holiday, or at weekends, etc.). The reason for this is that when our mind is free, it does better thinking. This is why you may well find that the idea for the scheme of work happens on the commute in the car, or, that the strategic plan you have been struggling with, suddenly forms while watching your kids swim on a Saturday morning. Sadly, despite how inconvenient this truth is, our brain does not want to only work in school hours. It can often produce the clearest thoughts when no one is asking it to.

Yet, in our school and work cultures, we don't really talk about this. If the head left the building at 4pm and said, 'I am going for a walk to think through a tricky problem' or 'I am going for a run to do some thinking on the development plan', would we think that this wasn't 'proper work'? If you're not quite ready to make that step, consider trying a meeting walking round the school site and focusing on an issue. For example, you could have a meeting with one of the SLT about 'school culture' where you both walk around the building and notice, observe, and record things. You may just find that the meeting comes alive! My very first headteacher did this all the time when I was a head of department; off we would go, walking around the building talking and observing. She would point things out to me and I to her. She was visible in school, and we spent time thinking and talking as we went, it was hugely valuable.

8. MAKE A START, HOWEVER SMALL!

If you are reading this thinking, 'I can't find three hours', then don't. Find one hour, put it in your diary, or protect it in your timetable if it is PPA, find somewhere quiet, turn off notifications and get into deep work, distraction free. No matter how little time you can find to start, find it, or nothing will ever change.

9. SHUT DOWN ROUTINES

Often, we do not shut down. We may finish and leave the school building but that does not mean we have shut down for the evening. Cal Newport suggests a 'shut down' routine every day in which we write down everything that needs to happen (some of which we may forget in the morning), re-evaluate the to do list, shut down all the open tabs on the computer, and then say, 'shut down completely until X'. Then we can be more present when we return home to see family or friends or simply do something relaxing for ourselves. While all this may sound dramatic, contrived, or awkward, the alternative is that we perhaps just never switch off. Teams who are not able to shut down and walk away will never be high performing in the long term. Burnt out leaders rarely have enough energy to light the flame in others.

> **Head Space: Thinking about your team**
>
> 1. Name the last time you had a stretch of 'deep work' time in working hours. What does this show you?
> 2. If all of your team had at least one slot of deep work a week, what would change?
> 3. When we are flitting, distracted between tasks, we do not produce our best work and instead, can feel exhausted and burnt out. What could you put in place to help you and your teams create time to do deep work?
> 4. What do staff feel about emails and the way they are used? What is helpful? What is a problem, and why?

CHAPTER 6:
HOW TO HELP PEOPLE FEEL SAFE AND BRAVE

In 'Team Psychological Safety' the word 'Team' is important. How the whole team feels about how safe they are as a group will determine how brave individuals are prepared to be. In turn that will shape both their team performance and that of the organisation. In most studies, people who work together closely share similar levels of psychological safety compared to people in other teams. Amy Edmondson's research has shown that psychological safety leads members of a team to feel more motivated, empowered, and less fearful of retribution. This means people are freer to voice their opinions and concerns, helps them to make better decisions, and encourages them to embrace mistakes and continually learn. If the team does not feel psychologically safe then there are significant consequences: stress, burnout, retention issues, as well as a lower standard of performance. It is impossible for most people to feel brave and take risks when they do not feel safe. Clearly, if we want to retain staff, develop people, enable them to be at the best more often, and to see the impact of their work, then we need to take this seriously.

WHY DO WE FIND THIS HARD?

What is psychological safety? How do we encourage a clear understanding of it in our teams, and, crucially, how do we approach achieving a work environment where we feel safe and so do our teams?

Edmondson is very clear about what psychological safety is and is not. Her research shows that in safe workspaces, people are:

- Not hindered by interpersonal fear.
- Willing to take the risk of being candid.
- More fearful of holding back than jumping in.
- Comfortable expressing and being themselves.
- Safe to share concerns and make mistakes without fear of retribution.
- Confident that they can speak up without being humiliated, ignored, or blamed.
- Happy to ask questions when they are not sure.
- Trusting and respectful of their colleagues.

Psychological safety is not the following things:

- It is not immunity from consequences.
- It is not about being 'nice'.
- It is not people having high self-regard.
- It is not about lowering standards.
- It is not about always being successful – people know that they might fail, and receive feedback on their performance explaining that they are not meeting expectations.
- It isn't being 'cosy' or a 'job for life' – people might lose their jobs for a number of reasons from changes in structure to their competency.
- It isn't about a lack of accountability – all workplaces have (and need) that.
- It is not about having no anxiety about the future.

In her book, *The Fearless Organisation,* Edmondson says, 'today's leaders must be willing to take on the job of driving fear out of the organisation to create the conditions for learning, innovation and growth'. It is clear that the most important factor in high performance and cohesive teams is psychological safety. But exactly how do we achieve that and how do we know when we have been successful?

MAKING IT HAPPEN – PRACTICAL IDEAS AND TOOLS

If people stay quiet until you ask them directly, then they are not yet feeling psychologically safe. As leaders, we are very vulnerable if people are sitting in our meetings or on our teams and thinking, 'I can't believe they are doing that, it will be a disaster' but do not feel they can say anything. People don't stay silent because they want you to make mistakes and fail, they stay silent because of their own fear. None of us want to be called disruptive or difficult, or to risk someone else thinking that we are questioning their authority. As a result, it takes a lot of deliberate work to get to the point where people feel they can take those interpersonal risks. How can we make this more likely? Announcing that we want people to feel psychologically safe, without understanding *how* we will encourage that, is a mistake.

1. CELEBRATE 'FAILURE' AND START REFRAMING

Most of us are great at this with young people but less good with ourselves! We know that we learn through failure, we know that to learn we have to take risks, and not all risks pay off. We know that to have our best ideas we need to be free to fail but … we don't like it. When we fail, we feel shame. When we feel shame, we hide. When we hide, we have to pretend. If we are pretending, we live in fear that someone will find out and expose us as the big failure we now think ourselves to be. This is not healthy for you, your school, or for your team. There are things we can do to help us start getting this right:

- **Define 'successful failure'.** Successful failure is when we have an idea, take some risks, plan it out, but then realise there are some things that are not going to work and so stop the plan happening before we go ahead, and it falls flat. Or when we put a proposal to the team and after discussion, we realise that the timeline or the idea is too ambitious, so we agree to change it. Google X don't refer to 'success' they refer to 'failing to fail'. If you can fail at the right time for the right reasons, then that *is a success*. We must get away from the notion that we have to follow through on everything we say, even if what we said now looks like a terrible idea!

- **Be open about when ideas have to die.** Due to embarrassment or a fear of looking incompetent, we sometimes keep going with ideas or plans that should have been stopped long ago. We try and wind things down as quietly as possible, so no one notices. It is interesting to see how Google X deals with ideas that need to die: they hold an annual celebration to hear testimonials about failed projects, even putting failed prototypes on a small altar, with people saying a few words about what the project meant to them. Employees report that this helps them dispose of the emotional baggage that they are carrying from investing so much of their time into something that didn't happen. I am not suggesting we go quite that far, but the principle is an important one: do we allow time to reflect on things that have not worked? When results have not gone up as we hoped, do we have a meeting to express how we feel, to talk about all the effort we put in? Do we help people process and acknowledge their emotions? Before we pick ourselves up and go again, we need a process to feel safe and brave again.

2. INVEST IN ONE TO ONES WITH DIRECT REPORTS

1:1 meetings are important to create psychological safety and to help people feel braver. There are some fundamental things that can be of help here:

- Rather than asking, 'How are you?', use this prompt: 'Take a moment to think about how things are going, based on that, how are things for you?' Ask people to give a RAG (Red, Amber, Green) rating or give an answer from 1 to 10. This is a more nuanced approach.

- Ensure that your team can bring their list of agenda points to you rather than it being a briefing to them from you. *You* may feel great if you have got through *your* list, but *they* are stuck, which isn't good!

- Ask the following questions:
  How can I help you?
  How are you doing/what is going well?
  What barriers/roadblocks/challenges are you facing? What is not going well?
  What do you need from me?
  How can I support you/what resources can I provide?

3. ASK POWERFUL QUESTIONS THAT YOU DON'T KNOW THE ANSWER TO ALREADY!

Asking powerful questions allows people to think deeply and also enables the asker to find out a whole range of things that they didn't know already. Sometimes we feel we should know all the answers and worry that someone may say we are incompetent if we admit that we don't. If we feel like that, we stop asking questions, stop showing vulnerability, and start pretending that we know everything. We need to swap that behaviour (which comes from fear) and embrace our inner 'don't knower'. Powerful questions (and powerful answers) happen when we ask questions that we *don't* know the answers to!

Powerful questions have important ingredients that makes them powerful, they:

- Show that you are interested in others' thoughts and feelings.
- Are thought provoking.
- Challenge assumptions.
- Generate energy and insights.
- Help focus people on the issues.
- Touch on deeper issues.
- Generate more questions.
- Don't have easy answers but encourage 'wondering' and reflection.

These are the types of questions that we should be ready to ask:

- What might we be missing?
- What are we assuming here?
- What other ideas could we generate?
- Who may have a different perspective?

- What leads you to think so?
- How do we know that this is true?
- What else do you feel about this situation?
- What are the other ways of getting to the same outcome?

4. MAKE IT MORE COMFORTABLE FOR PEOPLE TO GET FEEDBACK

Author and coach Marshall Goldsmith has a helpful technique called 'Feed Forward' which allows people to learn and grow without any fear of being criticised. However, it requires people to be brave enough to ask questions! The steps outlined below only take two minutes, but you then repeat them with four or five people so that the whole process takes around ten minutes. This exercise can be done across staff.

- Choose a behaviour you would like to change and would make a positive difference in your life (i.e. a work or habit focused behaviour).
- Describe this behaviour to your first colleague, e.g. 'I want to be better at creating buy in with staff'.
- The colleague you have asked then gives you two suggestions that might help that change happen, e.g. 'you could try and …', 'you would need to …'.
- Do not question or comment on these suggestions. Simply say 'thank you', as you make notes.
- Go to a new partner and repeat the process (and repeat four or five times).
- By the end you will have eight to ten suggestions from the people you work with about what you could do in the future to make a positive difference.

This technique is helpful in creating psychological safety because:

- We are helping people learn to be right, not telling them where they have been wrong.
- There is no judgement.
- It is not taken as personally as feedback often is.
- There is an assumption that change is possible.

- We are open to suggestions from our colleagues.
- It is a good, and safe way, of being more open about what we want to work on.
- It is low stakes and quick.

5. TRY THINKING PAIRS

Thinking Pairs is an exercise that coach and author Nancy Kline introduced and is very liberating once you get over the alien nature of what she is suggesting. For Thinking Pairs, you find a partner, set a timer for 15 minutes and then ask them this question, 'What would you like to think about and what are your thoughts?' You then simply listen without interrupting until the other person has nothing left to say. Then the listener asks, 'What more do you think, or feel, or want to say?' and keeps asking 'what more?' rather than interrupting or sharing their own thoughts. This technique allows other people to think for themselves, to feel safe but also to make themselves braver in the process. Once the first partner has listened for 15 minutes, you then switch roles.

> **Head Space: Thinking about your team**
>
> 1. What is your relationship with 'failure'? How safe and brave do you feel right now? What is stopping you from being braver?
> 2. When someone comes to you with some bad news, how do you make that a positive experience where they feel safe?
> 3. What have you done to destigmatise failure and what more could you do as a team to celebrate when you have learned from mistakes and acted?
> 4. How do you do feedback? What would need to change for people to feel safer and braver in your team?

CHAPTER 7:
HOW TO NOT MAKE THINGS WORSE

Clearly, none of us deliberately try and make things worse and yet sometimes that is exactly what we do. Sometimes we realise this in the moment ... when what we have just said or done has not had the intended reaction. Often, we only reflect after the moment and see it all unfolding in hindsight. Regretting these things can keep us awake at night, make us cringe at our own behaviour, and worry about how we will manage to rectify the situation. Whether it is an upset parent in reception or a team where there has been a rupture, we need to know how we can approach things to make them better and not worse. For that to happen though, we need to know how to pull situations back from the brink.

WHY IS THIS SO HARD?

In any pressurised situation or in the height of emotion, it is hard to think straight. As leaders, we face these situations all the time. We have to keep our heads, work out what is being said, what is not being said, and try and to respond in the right way. This process all happens so quickly that we are often not consciously aware of it; that is why it is hard. Add in feeling exhausted, feeling under pressure, feeling personally attacked, and not having enough time and the whole thing becomes even more difficult.

When we are placed in a difficult situation – or one that shouldn't be difficult but is because we are personally struggling – it is easy to become defensive and come across as arrogant. When we get defensive, we put on armour to protect ourselves and start attacking as a form of self-protection. This defensiveness can be subtle, but very rarely makes us feel better – it doesn't make the people on the receiving end feel good either. We can become arrogant, insisting that our way is right, our view is correct, and that we know the best thing to move things forwards. We might start telling people what they will do, what they need to understand, or start giving instructions and issuing orders. Think of the last altercation you had with a parent in school. Play it back in your mind as if you are a fly on the wall and look at what you see. Did you make it worse? You didn't mean to make it worse of course, but you may well have. Or think about a team meeting where something difficult was raised and you thought shutting it down was the best option at the time. Did people feel silenced? Did the incident leave them talking to each other in corridors about your reaction? Even with the best intentions, you may well have made it worse.

We all make mistakes. We are going to make the wrong calls, take the wrong approach, and sometimes show up with the wrong attitude. We are human and we are flawed but there are some things we can do that will help us feel less like our impulsive reactions are driving the bus. We might still find handling high stress situations hard (it is!), but we will at least have a roadmap for how to navigate them.

MAKING IT HAPPEN – PRACTICAL IDEAS AND TOOLS

1. ENSURE THAT YOU ARE 'OK'

If we don't want to make things worse for ourselves and for our teams, then we need to invest more of our time and energy into 'being OK'. This is easier said than done, I know. In education, we are not very good at this; we are so busy trying to make sure everyone else is OK, that we don't realise we are not in a healthy place ourselves. We often reward martyrdom and sacrifice, putting ourselves last and others first, often at great personal cost. The work of Frank Ernst helps us understand what happens when we are not OK. Ernst talks about four positions that we can find ourselves in:

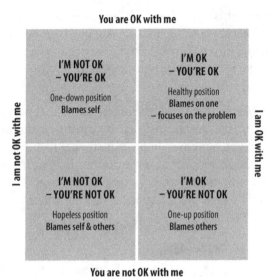

Figure 4: Ok Corral

I'm OK – you're OK (Healthy)

This is the position we are aiming for. It is when we are not blaming other people but focusing on the problem. When we are here, we have a belief that people are worthy and valuable. We have an honesty and openness that helps us to be collaborative and to engender trust. We are accepting of ourselves, knowing that we are flawed (as we all are!), but not having a civil war in our heads. When we are in this position, we are in control of ourselves. We can show 'Radical Candor', where we can both care and challenge and we are less likely to jump into rescue or condemn others (see *Radical Candor* by Kim Scott, and the first *Time to Think*). Our teams are more likely to thrive because we are thriving. We can take criticism without going into self-destruct mode and we can really listen to and understand others. High levels of trust lead to high levels of psychological safety and this feels good. We all need to get here!

I'm not OK – you're OK (One down)

This is the position when we start blaming ourselves. Our internal chatter takes centre stage and starts saying, 'I am not feeling OK, but other people seem to be just fine … so it must be me, I'm an idiot'. When we start going down this line of thought, our behaviour changes. We feel powerless and that leads to us discounting our own needs. We don't do the emotional and physical maintenance we need to do to keep ourselves OK, for example, we might stop taking breaks, tell ourselves we won't stop, or go to bed too late, etc.

It starts to feel like we don't have the power to make the changes we need to make and feel like we are the victim. If we feel like that in a team meeting, we start to emotionally leak. If we feel like this when dealing with an upset parent, we will become defensive. If we are challenged by a colleague, we will start blaming ourselves. When we lead from this position we start to feel out of control, and we make things worse for ourselves and for others.

I'm not OK – you're not OK (Hopeless)

In this position we are blaming both ourselves and others. We feel helpless and frustrated and start behaving in a way that is self-destructive. Emotional leakage has probably turned into a flood, and our teams are experiencing it. It is hard to face the brutal facts and have hope, it is hard to be objective, it is hard not to take everything personally, and it can start to feel hopeless. This is a struggle I address in the first *Time to Think*.

I'm OK – you're not OK (One up)

Here, we are blaming others but not ourselves. Although this may feel like a step forward from our own perspective, it is not helpful for either us or the people who we are blaming. If you have ever been on the receiving end of this dynamic, then you will know how awful it is. When we take the one up position, we are projecting our difficulties onto other people. We are critical, disdainful, and will start behaving with an air of superiority that others find irritating. We may get angry and blame others for problems. To make ourselves feel better, we will require someone else to feel worse. Of course, none of this is deliberate – we would never frame it like this to ourselves and even reading it feels awkward – but when we lead from this position, we will quickly run into problems and so will our team (many of whom are likely to be deeply unhappy and leave). We can and should challenge, of course, but when we do it from this position, it rarely goes well. Teams start to falter when leaders behave like this.

How do we get back into a healthy position? That comes down to what it is that *you* yourself need in your life to stay OK (in and out of work). List the things that make being OK more likely, and then check your diary to see where they are. You may find that if they are not explicitly scheduled in, then they just don't happen. As discussed above you are not the only one who is losing out. Whether it is running, surfing, walking, meeting friends, working out at the gym, a bath, a night away, a good book, getting up early, laughing, having a coffee in a coffee shop, playing games, journaling, mini breaks ... plan them out and do them. All of these things help to bring you perspective. All of these things will help you to feel and be better. Engaging in things that enable you to be OK is a win-win for everyone: you, your family, your friends, and your workplace.

2. AVOID DRAMA TRIANGLES

We are a profession that wants to help people; we want to make a difference, and we want to make things better. Ironically, in trying to make things better, sometimes we make them worse. Since the 1960s psychiatrist Stephen B. Karpman has used the Drama Triangle to illustrate how people relate to each other and how things can get worse as conflict arises – culminating in his book *A Game Free Life* (2014). It is particularly helpful to relate the Drama Triangle to the OK Corral and ask yourself whether your position on the first is different depending on how OK you are.

The Drama Triangle illustrates the roles that we take depending on our personality, our attitude, and our context. Karpman argues that we shift into a different role around the triangle if that move gives us power or helps us to feel better about ourselves. Sometimes we rationalise these moves (e.g. 'it's all your fault'). Of course, all of this can happen at lightning speed!

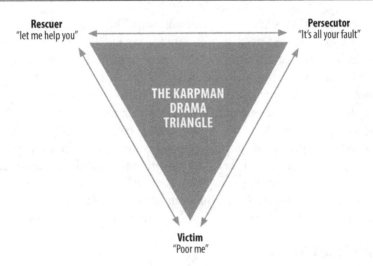

Figure 5: Drama Triangles

There are three positions on the triangle: the persecutor, the rescuer, and the victim. Karpman suggests that we all have a preferred position that we take during moments of tension or conflict, but we also switch roles as it suits us. When teams have had a fracture, then we will all take up these positions unless we find another way of communicating the issues. If we stay in a Drama Triangle when we have ruptures in our team, we will make things worse. We think we are benefitting from the position we take (and perhaps it appears we do initially) but it won't help to bring about a resolution.

It is helpful to explore what can happen when this plays out in our teams. Remember, we take a starting position but will often then change depending on people's reactions.

The persecutor position

If we are here, we may want to feel powerful and achieve that through blame, criticism, stepping in, and dominating. People can find this behaviour controlling or accuse us of being a bully. If we are accused of this, sometimes we can jump to being the victim. This position is a classic 'I'm OK, you're not OK'.

The victim position

If we take this position, then it may be because we feel powerless, hopeless, out of control, and at the mercy of the persecutor. We may complain, without taking action or moving things forward. If we feel that things are not fair and we are being unduly criticised, we may look to a rescuer to help us. This position is 'I'm not OK, you're not OK'.

The rescuer position

In this position, we may be a people pleaser; we may want to avoid conflict at any cost, or we may want to help, and we jump in to do so. There are many potential problems with this position. Firstly, the way we rescue encourages the victim to go further into victimhood. Secondly, the victim becomes even more helpless and dependent on us, and this doesn't help long term. Thirdly, we can get frustrated and end up becoming the victim or the persecutor. This leads to confusion, disappointment, and a breakdown of trust and relationships. We can find we are confused as events unfold and we move around the positions of both the Drama Triangle and the OK Corral.

3. FOCUS ON EMPOWERMENT NOT DRAMA

David Emerald, author and business leader, proposed an alternative to the Drama Triangle which moves it from a negative focus (identifying the problem) to a positive one (looking for solutions). If we have a natural position in the Drama Triangle, how can we move it to a positive position? He calls this The Empowerment Dynamic or The Empowerment Triangle. In this model, there are some important swaps to be made.

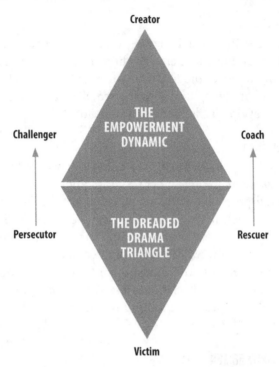

Figure 6: The Empowerment Dynamic

Persecutor becomes challenger

Instead of blaming we can ask better questions, use our ability to tell the truth, and call things out as a way of building up other people and helping them learn and grow. However, as a challenger, we must also care. Delivery is crucial to challenging with care: it must be more 'noticing' than 'judging'. For example, 'I notice that you/we sometimes make decisions that later we regret and have to undo, what is behind that do you think?', rather than, 'you are impulsive, and your bad decisions are causing us all to make mistakes'. We need challengers in the team so that we can all think differently. Challengers can hold people to account, but they must not become persecutors. If they do, we all lose.

Victim becomes creator

Here, we do not allow ourselves to be trapped by our circumstances but choose our response; learning to take action on those things under our control. We become focused on the change we want to make and find ways of implementing it. We see challenges not as something that will weigh us down but as barriers that can be overcome. In teams it is helpful to have people who are able to say, 'I am feeling under pressure, and this doesn't make sense to me'. If we can then turn that into, 'what may really help is …', then our teams are owning and creating their own change. They are empowered not dependent.

Rescuer becomes coach

Rather than allowing the victims to go even further into victimhood, helplessness, and dependency by saving them, we instead provide support to enable them to remove their own barriers. This is not achieved by doing it for them, nor is it done by telling them what you would do if you were in their position. The coach listens, asks great questions, stays silent more than they talk and allows people to shine in the spotlight of their attention, so that they can find their own solutions. Having good coaches in a team is far better than having people pleasers and rescuers.

If we can turn what may be a natural reaction to conflict or tension into something that strengthens us and our teams, we will all be better off.

> **Head Space: Thinking about your team**
>
> 1. What position are you currently sitting in on the OK Corral diagram? What are you going to do to move back into a healthy position? Write down the very first step.
> 2. As a team, how do people respond when there is conflict? In your mind's eye, play back the last 'rupture' you had as a team (even if it was small) and watch it like you are an observer. What do you notice about you and others?
> 3. What is your usual go to position on the Drama Triangle? What are the steps you might need to take to move from drama to empowerment?

CHAPTER 8:
HOW TO WORK WITH YES AND NO

Saying 'no' is an important part of being a leader, having boundaries, and being able to put your weight in the right place. In the first *Time to Think*, saying no without causing offence and owing our no got its own chapter. This chapter is about how we can use the power of no with our teams, and with parents, students, and other stakeholders.

Identifying how we can use other people's 'no' to get a better understanding of them and their situation is a crucial skill, but it is one that most of us are never taught. Hostage negotiators like Nicky Perfect (formerly with the MET Police) and Chris Voss (formerly FBI) understand the power of getting a no. They are trained in how to use this technique to negotiate, de-escalate, and to build empathy. As schools face more aggression from some areas of their communities, understanding how we can use some of these approaches may help us feel like things are more manageable.

We want to make the situation better, not worse. We may have to 'unlearn' some of the ways we have previously been operating so that we can get better outcomes. As Chris Voss says:

> Persuasion is not about how bright or smooth or forceful you are. It's about the other party convincing themselves that the solution you

want is their own idea. So don't beat them with logic or brute force. Ask them questions that open paths to your goals. It's not about you.

WHY DO WE FIND THIS HARD?

Very simply, learning how to say no is one thing, understanding how to work with other people saying no, and what they mean, is rather different. Hostage negotiators, and other similar professions, are taught listening, communication, and questioning skills so that when they are under pressure, they have the tools they need to bring about resolutions. They are told what to listen to and what to look out for, how to re-frame and how to re-phrase, and how to take the immediate risk out of situations. Of course, this is hard for those of us in education, as we have generally never had training like this! When we find an angry parent in reception, or a defiant student, we handle them the same way we always have done. The question to ask ourselves is, 'is that way working?' If it *is* then great (and it will be with some), but if it isn't, then perhaps we need to learn another way.

Chris Voss argues that 'no' does a lot of work and has a lot of skills. It can be as blunt and direct as a verbal 'no' or it can take the form of people not agreeing to do something. Other expressions like – 'I don't know', 'I'm not bothered', or 'I don't want to talk about it' – can all be forms of 'no'. In contrast, 'Yes' doesn't always mean yes, and this is why the best negotiators always aim to get a 'no'.

- 'No' allows the real issues to be unearthed.
- 'No' lets people make good decisions and protects them from making bad ones.
- 'No' slows things down so that people can really think about the decision and their agreement.
- 'No' helps people feel in control, safe, and more emotionally secure.
- 'No' moves us all forward through mutual understanding.

There are 3 types of 'yes'. They mean different things, but they all sound the same:

1. Counterfeit – 'I want to say no, but I have said yes'.
2. Confirmation – This is usually a response to a black and white question, rather than a firm commitment to action.
3. Commitment – 'My yes means yes.'

If we want to get a fully committed yes, then, ironically, first we have to get a no. How can we use this principle in our teams and with the people we work with?

MAKING IT HAPPEN – PRACTICAL IDEAS AND TOOLS

1. UNDERSTAND WHAT 'NO' MEANS

Chris Voss talks about 'no' as a technique in his book *Never Split the Difference*. In hostage negotiation, no is a great opportunity for both parties to understand what they don't want and what they do. Negotiators try to get someone to say 'no' to one of their questions because it gives them something to go on. We often think of a 'no' as defiance or unreasonableness, but Voss argues that it is the start of the negotiation, not the end of it. Great negotiators deliberately try to find a no because they understand that only then can the real negotiating begin.

'No' can mean:

- I am not ready to agree yet.
- You are making me feel uncomfortable.
- I don't understand.
- I want something else.
- I need more information.
- I want to talk it over with someone else.

2. EXPLORE A DIFFERENT STRUCTURE THAT ENABLES PEOPLE TO FEEL MORE IN CONTROL

Imagine (and this may not be hard) that you have a parent in reception who is demanding to see you. They are angry because you have sent a letter home regarding their child's behaviour. They think you are wrong, are being unfair and targeting their child, and say 'they won't be coming in to this school to be picked on'. We might well go into this situation prepared for battle. We may even think, 'I am right, you are wrong, you can't come into school behaving like this', and even tell them so. If we do, then they will likely get more and more angry, things will escalate, we will feel unsafe, and now we will have a stand-off in the school foyer in front of the reception team. We will call for back up on the radio and point to the notice on the reception window saying, 'we do not tolerate abuse of our staff'. Someone might even call the police, hoping the threat will encourage them to leave. We will then have to follow this unfortunate series of events up with a letter attaching the new parental behaviour policy and ban them from entering the school reception again. Sorted. Or is it? How will we move forward with this child or these parents? This kind of confrontation is going to happen again. We haven't learned anything about what is behind the problem in the first place.

Though the contexts and people will vary, in a conflict like this the situation will be driven by two main urges: the need to feel secure and safe, and the need to feel in control. If you can enable people to feel both of these things, then you have every chance of being able to find a resolution.

Those trained in negotiation use a process of discovery to find out as much as possible about the conflict and the person they are dealing with. Try these strategies:

- Stay silent for 90 seconds to allow your own freeze, flight, fight response time to subside. It takes time for you to get back in control; count in your head, take time to make a drink or engage in positive self-talk in your own mind. You will find you will feel calmer as a result.

- Acknowledge the negatives, 'I can see that this is really troubling you'. Ignoring the behaviour that someone is presenting to you doesn't help either party. Letting someone know that you see them lets them know that you are listening and being present with them.

- Ask them a question that helps them get control back, e.g. 'We can talk here now, or you could wait just a few moments and I can arrange a more private room, what would you prefer?' If they say no, that's OK, they are still telling you something about what they do and don't want. We can then ask about that and say, 'what is it about that that is not working for you?', 'is there anywhere else you would feel more comfortable?'

- Name the emotion. ("It *seems* like/it *looks* like/it *feels* like"). What we must not do is tell people how they are feeling because we don't know, and we could be wrong which will send the whole conversation in the wrong direction. Avoid saying, 'you are angry', 'you are upset', instead say, 'it feels like you are angry' or 'it looks like you are upset'. This approach allows the person to tell you how they are actually feeling instead of attacking you for your wrong labelling of their emotion.

- If someone says, 'no, I am not angry', you say 'I wasn't saying you were angry I was saying it looked like you were, if it isn't anger, what would you say you are feeling?'. We have to be careful how we label the emotion because we don't know what is happening for them and there are a range of feelings that display as anger; they may be frustrated, humiliated, disappointed, anxious and if we slap a label of 'angry' on them we won't find out what is causing the anger.

- Use tactical empathy – read their emotions and try to understand them. Avoid saying, 'I understand', it is highly unlikely that you do. Instead say, 'this must be so difficult, I really want to try and understand the situation'.

- Start the negotiation as discovery, not judgement. If we go into a conversation to tell people they are wrong without understanding how we find ourselves here, we are going to be no better off. The end point we are trying to get to may not change but how we get there is crucial. The conversation is a chance to understand what you have been missing so far, to be more curious as to what the problem is and to see a person as a human to be heard not simply a point on a to do list.

- Mirror and repeat phrases that they say, rather than putting words into their mouths, which can and risk misunderstanding or misrepresentation. Aim for no more than three words.

- Let silence do the heavy lifting – do not attempt to fill the silence, let them speak and think.

- Ensure that you keep a calm tone throughout.

3. ASK SOLUTION-BASED QUESTIONS TO UNPICK THE 'NO'

In high stakes situations and altercations, we sometimes don't ask any questions at all; we either attack or defend. Some of the questions below help to slow things down, reduce the level of emotion, and allow other people to feel heard and seen. We need to listen to what is being said here. If a parent comes to school three or four times, or repeatedly sends emails, then there is something that we are missing, and we need to find it out. Yes, having conversations is time consuming, but so is dealing with repeated calls and unexpected visits. The consequences of not having these conversations may well be far worse, as resentment builds and people criticise the school to others.

When you are next in a high-stakes conversation, try asking some of these questions:

- What do you *not* want?
- What about this is most important to you?
- What about this doesn't work for you?
- What would you need to make it work?
- It seems like there's something here that bothers you.
- How can I help to make this better for both of us?
- What am I missing here?
- Is there anything you want to say which would help me better understand?
- How do you want to feel at the end of this meeting?
- How would you like me to proceed?
- What is it that brought us into this situation?
- How can we solve this problem?
- What's the objective?
- What are we trying to accomplish here?
- How would I do that?

If you find that people don't want to answer these questions or speak, then Voss says that they are likely to be confused, indecisive, or have a hidden agenda. That position is very hard to shift, no matter what you do.

4. MAKE SOME SMALL CHANGES TO THE COMMON QUESTIONS WE ASK

Whether we are talking to our team members or to parents, there are ways of re-phrasing questions which will get us a better response while allowing the recipient of the question to feel in control. Voss recommends that anyone who wants to get better at negotiating uses the following four 'life changing' questions.

'Is now a bad time to talk?'

This question replaces, 'is now a good time to talk?' or 'have you got a few minutes to talk?' There are usually only two answers: 'not at all, now is a great time to talk' which means that you have their complete attention; or 'yes, it's a bad time, but how about X when I am free', which is also helpful because now you know you will have their full attention. When we phone parents, this can be a helpful strategy (unless the call is urgent!).

'Is this a ridiculous idea?'

Use this question instead of: 'is this a good idea?'; 'would you like to be part of X?'; 'would you be willing to …', etc. With those questions we often get a 'no but' answer. However, that *but* is often the most important thing that this person needs to tell you (and you need to understand). If you know what follows that 'but' then you are in a better place to bring solutions.

'Are you against …?'/'Do you disagree?'

We usually ask, 'do you agree?', or 'does this look like it will work for you?' These questions make a 'no' harder. As a result, you will not find out whether this person is really in or not. Reframing this question will get you nearer to clarity and commitment.

'Have you given up on …?'

We often ask things like 'do you still want to X?', or 'are you still wanting to move those assessments forward?'. It is better to check that the person we are asking has actually started (and that they actually wanted to start in the first place). This can be done with a question like, 'have you given up on the idea of writing the new assessments?'

If people have stopped communicating with you then it may be because you are either not listening to them and so they have given up trying to be heard, or they have lost influence and have given up. When people benefit from communicating with you, they continue to do so. If they have stopped it may suggest that they don't feel heard. If that is the case, you need to shift the communication techniques you are using.

One strategy to help people feel heard is to listen when people answer, summarise what you have heard them say, and then to ask them, 'is that right?' Only once they confirm should you move forward with a shared understanding. If they say 'no, that isn't right', then you have missed something and it is important to ask, 'what have I missed?'.

As school leaders (whatever stage we are at in our career), we engage in negotiations all of the time. Often, we are not conscious that this is what we are doing (or actually trained in negotiating constructive resolutions). We think reaching the 'yes' of agreement is the most important thing. However, without the ability to flush out the 'no', we often will not have a real understanding of why a problem has happened in the first place.

Head Space: Thinking about your team

1. How comfortable do you feel trying to get to the 'no' before the 'yes'? What is it about this new approach that feels uncomfortable for you?

2. Think back to an example of when a meeting with a parent or student hasn't gone well. How might some of these strategies have helped bring that to a different conclusion?

3. To do all of this well, we have to be able to listen intently, and be present, so that we don't miss anything. How can we ensure that we are able to do that?

4. If your team adopted these approaches and became skilled in listening, getting a no, and confirming the yes, what difference would it make in your team's interactions with angry or upset parents?

CHAPTER 9:
HOW TO EMPOWER BOTH EXTROVERTS AND INTROVERTS

We are all different. Understanding and harnessing that difference is what creates high performing teams. The way things operate in education often favours extroverts, and sometimes we miss out on brilliant people or ideas because we expect things to appear in a set way. If we want to be leaders who hear all viewpoints, we must listen to everyone, not just the people who shout the loudest. We must also understand that although someone who is more introverted may not enter into a debate in the same way as an extrovert might, that doesn't mean that they are not thinking or engaging. We cannot afford to marginalise the introverts in our teams or to misunderstand how they think and work. That said, we also need to utilise the extroverts so that they too can contribute and feel fulfilled. Getting this right with the people on our teams really does matter.

WHY DO WE FIND THIS HARD?

We find it hard not to favour the extrovert ideal. In her book *Quiet*, Susan Cain argues that this extrovert ideal has been promoted since the rise of industrialisation in America in the late nineteenth century, and society has come to favour charismatic, sociable, and outgoing leaders. In education there are elements of this too: extroverts enjoy the spotlight, the social status (measured by the number of 'followers' on social media platforms), and the buzz of being surrounded by lots of people and the stimulation that provides. Many of our recruitment procedures favour the extrovert: taking assemblies or lessons, meeting panels of students and staff and having to be sociable and high energy, presentations to a panel with less than an hour's preparation, and then open questions that could ask anything. We have student panels but often the things we are asking them to look for favour extroverts and are not always indications of the best teacher. Trying to think through practices like this that we have been doing for years, is hard.

It is also hard because we don't really understand the nuances of introversion and extroversion. We can do various personality tests (and some people find this helpful) but we also need to think about our structures and what we are inadvertently promoting and overlooking. Often, we say that people who are introverted are 'shy', but being shy is not the same as being an introvert.

Cain, an introvert herself, says that introversion is more about the way you respond to stimulation (including social stimulation). Introverts often feel most alive and their most capable and fulfilled when they are in quieter low-key environments. They sometimes prefer listening over talking and thinking before speaking. They may prefer observing what is happening rather than seeking attention from the group. Many introverts enjoy deep and thoughtful conversations and discussions, perhaps enjoy working alone, and often strongly dislike conflict. They do not like feeling overstimulated by busy, noisy environments. However, introverts can also 'flip the switch' and behave like extroverts, they may even appear to be one at times. That is why introversion can be hard to see if we do not know people well.

Extroverts, on the other hand, are outgoing, sociable, exuberant and enjoy the buzz of people and the stimulation that brings. They may enjoy the spotlight, need to be surrounded by people, enjoy acknowledgement from others and often strive for quick successes. Everyone is somewhere on the spectrum of introversion to extroversion; some people are both (ambiverts). It is sometimes hard even talking in these terms because there are so many factors that make up someone's personality and behaviour in different contexts, and human beings also change and adapt. No human being is one thing *or* the other, we are all a complex mixture of many factors.

All of us, whatever persuasion we generally inhabit, can also flip the switch. Our jobs frequently require us to act out of character for the good of the team or the school. If you are a head and you are an introvert, you know that you will have to flip the switch and be very sociable at open evenings and parents' evenings. If you a head and an extrovert, there will be times when you have to think deeply, alone, about some big decisions. Acting out of character for periods like this is something that we all have to do, however hard and uncomfortable it may feel. How do we manage these demands and remain ourselves? How can we create teams where both our introverted and extroverted sides thrive?

MAKING IT HAPPEN – PRACTICAL IDEAS AND TOOLS

1. CREATING 'RESTORATIVE NICHES'

The best way to continue to lead *and* be yourself is to create a 'restorative niche'. This concept comes from the work of Brian Little who used the term to refer to 'a place you want to return to be your true self'. This could be a physical place, or the practice of taking quiet breaks between meetings or lessons. Sometimes, when we know that we have something big coming up, we need to go a little easier in the days running up to it so that we are at our best – this is also a form of restorative niche. For example, if an introvert knows that they have a week of school open evenings coming up, they might decide to leave school earlier on the days before hand to help build up their capacity. Restorative niches can happen in the middle of lessons, or meetings, or break duties; they are times when we deliberately find a moment of internal calm and reflection. It is perfectly possible for introverts to act as extroverts when they know they need to, but this can be draining. There are many gifted teachers and leaders who act out of character in this way, because they love the job and love young people. To continue to be able to do this – and be brilliant at it – it helps if they are allowed and empowered to create their own restorative niches.

2. WE NEED TO KNOW HOW WE OPERATE

We need to understand what it is that we really love to do; the purposes that feel like we are at home. If we understand what lights us up as an introvert or an extrovert, and why, then we have found something that energises us, and a space where we can be more ourselves. In turn, this will help us feel more fulfilled. The same is true of understanding our colleagues and how they operate. Susan Cain suggests three questions to ask ourselves.

'What did you want to be when you were growing up?'

Think back to what you loved to do as a child. What job did you see yourself doing as an adult? Cain argues that while the specific profession you identified with may not have been right; the underlying impulse often was. If you wanted to be a firefighter, was that because you loved the idea of heroism and danger, because you wanted to operate the machinery, or because you liked the adrenaline of the unknown? If you wanted to be a teacher, was that because you loved instructing others, you loved the relationships with young people, or you liked the element of performance? You can find out a lot about yourself by thinking back.

Pay attention to the work you are gravitating towards

Are you offering to work with certain types of students? Do you prefer working with students who love your subject, or do you like the challenge of those who don't? Do you love planning the taught curriculum, or do you gravitate to the curriculum that happens in between lessons?

What do you envy?

Jealousy is an unpleasant emotion, but it can tell you some hard truths. We are jealous if someone has something we want: so, what is it that makes you jealous? What is it *they* are doing that *you* want to do? Being honest with yourself can help you to see what you actually want with greater clarity.

If our teams can be honest enough about these things, then we as leaders have a better chance of placing them where they feel the most themselves. If we can manage that then we will see people really thriving.

3. RE-THINK THE SPEED OF OUR DECISION MAKING (ESPECIALLY IN MEETINGS)

Introverts tend to want to think about 'what if' and extroverts tend to want to think about 'what is'. Often the pressure to move rapidly through the agenda in meetings means that they serve the extrovert ideal, where we are all happy to make decisions at lightning speed (based on 'what is') and then move things forward at pace. Although extroverts will find this energising and fulfilling, it is very likely that the introverts in the team feel a level of anxiety which will stop them from giving their best, or the team benefitting from their contribution. We need to slow things down and create time for all of us to reflect. There are some things we can do to help introverts to bring their best:

a. Share pre-reading in good time before the meeting so that people can understand the issues and think before they attend.

b. Run iterative meetings where you state that decisions *will not* be made. Rather, the aim is to explore the situation week on week until understanding grows.

c. Have a cool down period after decisions; sometimes we make decisions but the introverts, once they have thought deeply about it, will come back with some questions or reflections. Allowing a cool down period of a few days (or longer) on big decisions, will enable people to come back to you with other thoughts which may help make better decisions.

4. GROUP BRAINSTORMING ONLINE

Research around the power of online group collaboration has found that properly managed groups that brainstormed electronically did so better than individuals. Surprisingly, the larger the group, the better it performs. Research has also found that academic researchers who work together electronically, who are geographically separated, tend to produce research that is more influential than both those working alone or face to face.

Psychologists believe that brainstorming face to face has three limitations:

a. Social loafing – individuals sit back and let others take the reins.

b. Production blocking – only one person can take an idea at a time, everyone else sits passively.

c. Evaluation apprehension – the fear of looking stupid in front of others.

How could we maximise this insight with the staff in our schools, and avoid sticking to inefficient work and interviewing practices simply because of habit?

5. RE-EXAMINE YOUR INTERVIEW PROCESS

Look again at your process and ask the question, 'does this favour extroverts?' Although introvert candidates may well adapt to a process that favours extroverts, you may not get the best out of them and therefore not make the best hiring decisions. There are some things you can do about this:

- Think about your brainstorming activities. For the three reasons mentioned above, those activities often don't elicit the quality of a candidate's thinking. They often really show how extroverted people are good under pressure and enjoy the buzz.

- Think about what criteria young people are being asked to use to judge a candidate – do they favour the more charismatic and those who enjoy the buzz of the unknown?

- Consider whether giving interview questions in advance would help show all candidates at their best.

- When you are deciding on the tasks in interview, be very clear on what you are testing. It may be that your tasks favour the extroverts and are playing to their natural strengths, while disadvantaging those who are more introverted.

- You might even consider asking candidates about how they work and how to get the best out of them at the interview so that all your candidates are able to present the best of themselves.

6. ENSURE THERE IS CHANCE FOR DELIBERATE PRACTICE FOR ALL

In an influential series of studies K. Anders Ericsson posited that one of the things that unites many top performers, across disciplines, was 'deliberate practice' where time is spent in solitary practice of individualised training activities designed by a coach. The benefits of deliberate practice are well documented in educational circles now but *how* we do it is perhaps more elusive. Deliberate practice and coaching can help to identify the things that we don't know or can't do yet and give us a roadmap to learning them. We can then assess how we are performing and change what we are doing accordingly. That is how learning works. Once you have the input of a coach or teacher practice should be solitary as:

- You need intense concentration and no distractions.
- You need to develop a deep and personal motivation.
- You need to work on the task that is most challenging to you personally.

We have addressed how 'deep work' can be utilised for staff in another chapter dedicated to that topic, but what about students? How often do students work alone, in silence, on the things that they alone need to master? Introverted students may need this especially. We all know the challenges of around solitary silent work (behaviour, classroom management, different pedagogical approaches, etc.) but if our young people do not get to practice doing this kind of work at school, they will find it challenging when it comes to revision for exams and may struggle to manage the freedom of further education and the world of work.

Head Space: Thinking about your team

1. Where are you on the introversion-extroversion spectrum and how do you manage that so that you are at your best?
2. Does the way you currently run things lean towards the extrovert ideal? If so, what will you do to enable everyone in your team to thrive and have the chance to show their brilliance?
3. How much deliberate practice is happening in classrooms: for staff, for students, and for you?

CHAPTER 10:
HOW TO LEAVE WELL AND HELP OTHERS TO LEAVE WELL

Starting well and leaving well is important to all of us – as well as our families, and the schools we are working in – and negative experiences can have a lasting impact on our professional and emotional lives. 'Leave well' should be a mantra that we carry with us and aim for any time we leave a workplace. However, we should not be naïve as we explore this topic, we all know that people leave for a number of complex positive and negative reasons: health issues, work/life balance, as a result of disciplinary procedures, competence concerns, a change in governance, a change in leadership, being poached, redundancy or re-structures, not being aligned to the school culture, for promotion, or for a re-location. The reasons for people leaving are varied. I am not going to cover the rights and wrongs of any of this nor am I going to discuss anything relating to HR processes. I am going to explore how, no matter what the circumstances, we can leave *well* and how we can (as far as it is in our control) allow people to leave with their dignity intact. This matters because leaving any workplace, no matter what the reason, is a significant moment in our lives. We invest so much in a place that moving on can bring up all kinds of mixed emotions.

WHY DO WE FIND THIS HARD?

Making the decision to leave is often difficult and time consuming. Often, we are not able to leave as quickly as we may have planned. Due to the nature of the school set up, every time that you are interviewed you will have to tell someone that you are out of school, since you cannot take annual leave and cover needs to be arranged. Going out for interview can feel like a public thing and not getting the job can therefore also feel quite exposing (even if you didn't actually want it or pulled out!). Then, once you know for sure that you are leaving, you have the process of handing over – finishing one job with your mind already on the next. You are leaving behind young people who may be mid KS2, GCSE, or A level, and you know the disruption that it will cause to them. You have built relationships that you are walking away from. You know that the quality of the person in front of each child makes a significant difference to what that they can achieve, and you have worked hard to live up to that responsibility. It is hard because sometimes you feel guilty.

Seen from the other side of the fence, when someone tells you they are leaving, it also creates a reaction. You can understand why they need to do it, but still be worried about the process of replacing them and fearful about the problem this leaves you with. You will also have to process your own emotions if people are leaving under difficult circumstances, knowing that you may have been part of the reason they are leaving and that you may have had to do some difficult things.

On both sides, in whatever context, leaving is hard and we need to understand more about how we can make it better for both parties so that people can leave well.

The ideas below are for 'normal' leaving, when someone decides they want to move on or where leaving is mutually agreed as the right option. I am not going to cover when leaving becomes a complex and legal matter (unfair dismissal, whistleblowing, etc.) because these situations are so individual and contextual.

MAKING IT HAPPEN - PRACTICAL IDEAS AND TOOLS

If you are leaving (or hoping to leave), you will have told your line manager/CEO/head. As you prepare for this process, think about the following.

1. BE CLEAR ON THE NARRATIVE

Whatever the circumstances of your leaving, you need to choose your narrative and think about how you are going to transition over the next few weeks and months. How you do this says something about your character; what do you want your behaviour to 'say' about you? This requires sensitivity and planning and often we do not give it the time it deserves. It is worth some time investment to write the narrative arc of your time at the school and to make sense of why you are leaving. Depending on the context, your public narrative may or may not be able to be the whole truth. However, it is important that the narrative is one that you can stand by and that it is truthful. We don't have to tell people deeply personal details if we do not want to, we just need to find a narrative that we believe in. Len Schlesinger, co-author of *Just Start*, talks about the 'bookends' of a job, how we start and how we end really matter. Sometimes we need to re-frame: it can be the case that the reasons we are leaving is because there has been an issue that neither party can overcome, or there is a tension that cannot be resolved, but telling everyone that isn't always going to serve anyone well. It is important that you know how you are going to handle these dynamics and then establish for yourself the limits of what you are going to say.

2. WATCH YOUR WORDS!

Schlesinger says, 'there are no secrets and no off-the-record conversations in the workplace'. If you tell different people different things it will create controversy and speculation. Schlesinger advises, 'learn the essential lesson of being a politician: there is only one story, told one way ... stick to it, that way nobody can ever say they heard anything different'. Sometimes this needs to be agreed between you and your line manager, other times it is entirely your story to tell. Using the opportunity of leaving to snipe or to lob metaphorical hand grenades into the fray rarely ends well, even if what you are saying may be true. You cannot control the reactions of others or what they say, but you can control what you say. Working out the timing of what is going to be said and to whom is also important. Try to control the message and where it lands.

3. LEAVE YOUR JOB IN A GOOD PLACE

When you know that you are leaving, it is good to ensure that you will leave well; there is a handover, you leave showing your professionalism, and you don't leave loose ends which will cause others real problems. Educational circles are small; you will want to know that you have done all you can to leave the young people, your team, and the school in a good place. Sometimes, when leaving is sudden, this is not possible but over a 'normal' notice period, this is something that should be factored in.

4. EXPRESS GRATITUDE (AND BE CAREFUL IN EXIT INTERVIEWS)

Having a moment with your line manager towards the end of your time in a school is important. This can take many forms: a meeting with you and your line manager, a department/team meal, leaving speeches and gifts are the usual things that we tend to do. People can express their gratitude to you and you them. We need to end things well and this can do that as we mark the transition.

Some schools and Trusts conduct exit interviews. This can be a tricky one to navigate and depends on a number of contextual factors. It is tempting to use these interviews as a time to vent all that is wrong with the school, but Schlesinger argues that 'the exit interview is not the time to give the feedback you wished you had given while you were a full-time employee'. Firstly, you are not guaranteed anonymity, and it is a small world. Secondly, your feedback is not going to change the organisation *unless* the people conducting the interview really do want to hear your thoughts. We should feel safe and brave enough to give honest feedback before it comes to needing to leave but that largely depends on the culture of the school, your relationships, and whether feedback is taken seriously.

In 2022, 40,000 teachers left the state-funded sector (9% of the workforce), a further 4000 teachers retired. Clearly, this is a problem that isn't going away, and as school leaders we have to be prepared to manage it. Of course, we want people to stay, but if they still choose to leave then we need to make it the best experience that we can.

IF YOU ARE MANAGING SOMEONE ELSE LEAVING

1. CONTINUE TO COMMUNICATE WITH THEM WHILE THEY ARE STILL WITH YOU

If you have ever left a school and felt totally excluded, you will know how important it is to strike the right balance. Of course, people understand that they will no longer be involved in planning for the future or discussions that are no longer relevant, but that is rather different to feeling ignored. Do continue to check in and make sure that the leaver is OK and are still part of the team while they are here.

2. TALK ABOUT THE TRANSITION

Often the transition is not explicitly talked through and that can cause a lack of clarity. When someone tells you that they are leaving, it is helpful to discuss both what *they* feel is important to leave well, and what *you* would like them to complete before they go. Yes, it may be a little awkward but if the intention is that they leave well and things are left well, then there is common ground.

3. KNOW THEIR NARRATIVE

We may know the real reason why people are leaving; however, these reasons may be deeply personal and sensitive. It is important that we know what the leaver wants to say, and that we agree the public narrative together. When there are two (or more!) narratives doing the rounds, rumours and speculation starts and that is rarely helpful.

4. ALLOW THEM TO LEAVE WITH THEIR DIGNITY IN TACT

This one is important. Ask them what leaving well looks like. Some people want to make speeches, others don't, some like a big do, others would prefer a department meal, some like the fuss, some avoid it. Where the leaving has happened under sensitive circumstances, we need to particularly be aware of how we can allow people dignity. For example, if a temporary candidate has gone for a permanent job and lost out to an external candidate as their contract ends, that is a different context to someone who is leaving for promotion or to get married or to be nearer their family. Always write a card with some words that mean something in it; while these things appear small, they are not.

5. NORMALISE LEAVING

Leaving is a normal part of team development. That does not mean that there is not potential sadness as a team disbands. We can help to manage these emotions by acknowledging the changes, recognising the team and the individual's efforts and reflecting on what has been. The best approach is to acknowledge change, reflect, and learn, and then when we eventually leave ourselves, the team will change again. Whatever we feel about it, and whatever the context, leaving (or handling other people leaving) is part of being in a team.

Head Space: Thinking about your team

1. Think about your own leaving experiences, how were they handled? Which of the steps above would have been helpful for you?

2. How do you handle people leaving? Is there anything you need to put in place to do this better?

3. Think about your team now. What steps could you take to normalise leaving as a natural part of the team's lifecycle?

FINAL THOUGHTS

One of the interesting things about writing a book about leading teams is that you become very aware of your own leadership failings and faults. If you have read this book and thought, 'I don't do that as much anymore', or 'I haven't done that as well as I could have', then let me tell you that this is exactly how I felt writing it too! We are always learning, reflecting, and adapting our approach as our confidence and experience grows. I think it would be odd if we looked back over a career and felt that we had nailed everything we had laid our hands on. It would also be delusional because even if you think you have done a pretty great job, there is no guarantee that the team you are working with would agree.

I hope that you have also read this book and realised all the things that you *already do*. Each of us is finding our own way, grappling with the issues which present themselves in real time, and doing the best we can with what we have got. We are navigating leadership paradoxes that seem contradictory and yet we have to make our home in the heart of them.

In leading our teams, we must:

- Trust people *and* verify what we are being told is the truth.
- Give people autonomy *and* be clear about the boundaries that exist.
- Give everyone a voice *and* make it clear that not everyone gets a vote.
- Be responsible so that we are not reckless *and* be daring enough that we don't play it too safe.
- Know that what we are doing is right *and* be prepared to be wrong.
- Say 'I am doing everything I can think of' *and* accept that we won't have thought of everything.

- Be humble enough to know we need others *and* have enough belief that we can pull things off.

As leaders, we spend much of our time wondering if we have missed the boat (or are sinking it!). Perhaps we need to spend more time thinking about how we are steering the boat and where it is going. We need to think about who is on board and how we can make things work for all of us, so that success is inevitable, and we arrive at the right destination. Sometimes this is hard and sometimes we feel stuck. I hope that if you feel like that then this book has given you a way through.

As leaders, we lead. Followers should not follow blindly. Our job is to instil enough confidence in our teams that they *want* to follow, so that they feel safe and brave, and so that they too can be responsibly daring. To help them, we must model what that looks like, and at times when our schools need us to be more daring than we are naturally comfortable with, we sometimes need to hold our nerve. All of us are learning as we go, making mistakes, trying new things, wanting to be better tomorrow than we were today, and being the kind of leaders that people want to follow. It's a lifetime of discovery, we might never know it all, but we know more today than we did yesterday and that is progress. Look ahead towards the future but don't forget to look back and see how far you have come.

ACKNOWLEDGEMENTS

I have been fortunate to be part of, and witness, many great teams in my life so far. Being in these teams has helped me work out my own leadership in real time and make mistakes that might have felt hard when I made them but have been valuable to me.

To my friendship team: those people who have been on my side for many years now and continue to be there through the ups and the downs of life, thank you for helping me feel safe enough to be brave. My hut girls, this last year has been on another level but so has your friendship. Mel (aka Diana), my first partner in crime and my longest standing friend who has been there through it all. Joe, you continue to help me feel safe and brave, what a gift that is. To Gill, Simon, and Jenny, who rescue my children when I am on a late running train, make sure I don't forget crucial things like school trips and non-uniform days, and make me laugh as we attempt to bring up small humans in a complex world. To Rach, you could go in the family section but since I would have chosen you as my friend if we weren't related, you belong here too. Thanks for watching out for us.

I'm grateful for the teams I have led and worked in over the years, from the patience of colleagues as I learned the ropes in my early Head of Department days to the PiXL team who are working together to do something brilliant in service to schools. To my PiXL Leadership Team who care for and challenge me and each other so brilliantly, I'm so proud of you and us. The words in this book are all the things we have discovered together and continue to explore every day. The work is never done!

To my family team: Paul, Charlotte, Daniel, and Matthew, you will always get a mention in anything I do because you allow me to do it. Thank you for accepting who I am and what I want to do and backing me every step of the way, even when some of it involves compromise.

A final thanks to three individuals, without whom, I don't think any of this would be possible: Karen, thanks for creating order out of disorder, you see my relieved face each week! Anders, thank you for your clarity, precision, and speed, you're a pleasure to work with. Emma, I do not know how I managed without you. Thank you for organising me, supporting me, believing that it is possible when the length of the to do list suggests otherwise, and for knowing that my 'deep work' time is sacred. You are a pleasure to work with and I am so glad you are here.

In every book I buy, I always turn to the acknowledgements first. If you do this or have made it to the end, I would like to acknowledge you, the reader of this book. Thank you for buying it, for being curious enough to read it, and for the appetite you clearly have to lead and to learn. I hope what you have read helps you be the leader you want to be.

REFERENCES

Adams, Richard, 'Record numbers of teachers in England quitting profession'. *The Guardian*. Available at: https://www.theguardian.com/education/2023/jun/08/teachers-england-schools-figures-department-education-survey.

Andersen, Jens (2022). *The LEGO Story: How a Little Toy Sparked the World's Imagination*. Mariner Books.

Brighouse, Tim, & David Woods (2006). *Inspirations: A Collection of Commentaries and Quotations to Promote School Improvement*. Network Continuum Education.

Brown, Juanita, Issacs, David, & Nancy Margulies (1999). 'Asking Big Questions: A Catalyst for Strategy Evolution', available at: https://theworldcafe.com/wp-content/uploads/2015/07/askingbig.pdf.

Buckingham, Marcus, & Ashley Goodall (2019). *Nine Lies About Work: A Freethinking Leader's Guide to the Real World*. Harvard Business Review Press.

Cain, Susan (2013). *Quiet: The Power of Introverts in a World That Can't Stop Talking*. Penguin.

Carucci, Ron & Kathleen Hogan (2022). '6 Ways to Reenergize a Depleted Team'. *Harvard Business Review*. Available at: https://hbr.org/2022/11/6-ways-to-reenergize-a-depleted-team.

Collins, Jim (2001). *Good to Great*. Random House.

Covey, Sean, Huling, Jim & Chris McChesney, (2012). *The 4 Disciplines of Execution*. Free Press.

Crowe, John, Andrew Allen, Joseph & Nale Lehmann-Willenbrock (2016). 'Humor in Workgroups and Teams'. In *The Psychology of Humor at Work*, ed. Christopher Robert, Taylor & Francis, pp. 96-108. Available at: https://www.researchgate.net/publication/308519609_Humor_in_Workgroups_and_.

Womeldorff, David Emerald (2009). *The Empowerment Triangle – The Power of TED: The Empowerment Dynamic*. Polaris.

Edmondson, Amy C. (2018). *The Fearless Organization: Creating Psychological Safety in the Workplace for Learning, Innovation, and Growth*. Wiley.

Ericsson, K. A., Krampe, R. T. & C. Tesch-Römer (1993). 'The role of deliberate practice in the acquisition of expert performance'. *Psychological Review*. DOI: 100 363–406. 10.1037/0033-295x.100.3.363.

Ernst, Franklin H. (1971). 'OK Corral: Grid for Get-On-With' *Transactional Analysis Journal* (1:4). DOI: 10.1177/036215377100100409.

Fried, Jason (2012). 'Why Work Does not Happen at Work'. *TEDxMidwest*. Available at: https://www.youtube.com/watch?v=0UmUgaJwEr0.

Goldsmith, Marshall, 'Try Feedforward Instead of Feedback', available at: https://marshallgoldsmith.com/articles/try-feedforward-instead-feedback/.

Herold, Cameron (2016). *Meetings Suck*. Lioncrest Publishing.

Holmes, Cassie (2024). *Happier Hour: How to Spend Your Time for a Better, More Meaningful Life*. Penguin Life.

Hughes, Damian (2018). *The Barcelona Way: How to Create a High-Performance Culture*. Macmillan.

Karpman, Stephen B. (2014). *A Game Free Life: The new transactional analysis of intimacy, openness, and happiness*. Drama Triangle Publications.

Kline, Nancy (2002). *Time to Think: Listening to Ignite the Human Mind*. Cassell.

Kline, Nancy (2015). *More Time to Think: The Power of Independent Thinking*. Cassell.

Knight, Rebecca (2014). 'How to Quit Your Job Without Burning Bridges'. *Harvard Business Review*. Available at: https://hbr.org/2014/12/how-to-quit-your-job-without-burning-bridges.

Lencioni, Patrick (2002). *The Five Dysfunctions of a Team: A Leadership Fable.* John Wiley & Sons.

Lencioni, Patrick (2004). *Death by Meeting: A Leadership Fable About Solving the Most Painful Problem in Business.* Jossey-Bass.

Lencioni, Patrick (2022). *The 6 Types of Working Genius: A Better Way to Understand Your Gifts, Your Frustrations, and your Team.* Matt Holt.

Newport, Cal (2016). *Deep Work: Rules for Focused Success in a Distracted World.* Piatkus.

Perfect, Nicky (2023). *Crisis: True Stories of my Life as a Hostage Negotiator.* HQ.

Rogelberg, Steven G. (2024). *Glad We Met: The Art and Science of 1:1 Meetings.* OUP USA.

Schlesinger, Leonard A. & Charles. F Kiefer (2012). *Just Start: Take Action, Embrace Uncertainty, Create the Future.* Harvard Business Review Press.

Scott, Kim (2019). *Radical Candor: How to Get What You Want by Saying What You Mean.* Pan.

Smith, Wendy K. & Marianne W. Lewis (2022). *Both/And Thinking: Embracing Creative Tensions to Solve Your Toughest Problems.* Harvard Business Review Press.

Sparks, Joe & Rachel Johnson, 'The PiXL Change In Us Checklist'.

Stewart, Ian & Vann Joines (2012). *T A Today: A New Introduction to Transactional Analysis.* Lifespace Publishing.

Voss, Chris (2017). *Never Split the Difference: Negotiating as if Your Life Depended on It.* Random House Business.

Voss, Chris (2023). 'Negotiation Training: The Top 4 'No-Oriented' Questions'. *The Black Swan Group* (blog). Available at: https://www.blackswanltd.com/the-edge/negotiation-training-the-top-4-no-oriented-questions?hs_amp=true.

Walters Cohen, Amy (2023). *Ruthlessly Caring: And Other Paradoxical Mindsets Leaders Need to be Future-Fit.* Wiley.

West, Chris (2020). *The Karpman Drama Triangle Explained: A Guide for Coaches, Managers, Trainers, Therapists – and Everybody Else.* CWTK Publications.

'Resolving Conflict with the Drama and Empowerment Triangles', *The profit recipe* (blog), available at: https://theprofitrecipe.com/blog/drama-triangle-and-empowerment-dynamic.